CHICAGO PUBLIC LIBRARY

W9-CDO-135

DISCARD

DATE DUE

MAR 1 8 2005			

DEMCO 38-296

DISCARD

Oriole Park Branch
7454 W. Balmoral Ave.
Chicago, IL 60656

Hitler's Henchmen

By Marylou Morano Kjelle

LUCENT BOOKS®

San Diego • Detroit • New York • San Francisco • Cleveland
New Haven, Conn. • Waterville, Maine • London • Munich

On cover: Nazis on trial at Nuremberg (center); Heinrich Himmler (upper left); Joseph Goebbels (upper right); Baldur von Schirach (lower left); Rudolf Hess (lower right).

© 2003 by Lucent Books. Lucent Books is an imprint of The Gale Group, Inc., a division of Thomson Learning, Inc.

Lucent Books® and Thomson Learning™ are trademarks used herein under license.

For more information, contact
Lucent Books
27500 Drake Rd.
Farmington Hills, MI 48331-3535
Or you can visit our Internet site at http://www.gale.com

ALL RIGHTS RESERVED.
No part of this work covered by the copyright hereon may be reproduced or used in any form or by any means—graphic, electronic, or mechanical, including photocopying, recording, taping, Web distribution or information storage retrieval systems—without the written permission of the publisher.

LIBRARY OF CONGRESS CATALOGING-IN-PUBLICATION DATA

Kjelle, Marylou Morano.
Hitler's henchmen / by Marylou Morano Kjelle.
p. cm. — (History makers)
Summary: Profiles five men who held positions of power in Hitler's regime, reviewing their service to the Third Reich and pointing out the personality defects that made them invaluable to their leader.
Includes bibliographical references and index.
ISBN 1-59018-229-4 (alk. paper)
[1. Nazis—Biography—Juvenile literature. 2. National socialism—Juvenile literature. 3. Hitler, Adolf, 1889–1945. 4. Germany—Politics and government—1933–1945.]
I. Title. II. Series.
DD243.K54 2003
943.086'092'2—dc21

2002011839

Printed in the United States of America

R03003 00584

CONTENTS

DISCARD

Oriole Park Branch
7454 W. Balmoral Ave.
Chicago, IL 60656

FOREWORD

The literary form most often referred to as "multiple biography" was perfected in the first century A.D. by Plutarch, a perceptive and talented moralist and historian who hailed from the small town of Chaeronea in central Greece. His most famous work, *Parallel Lives*, consists of a long series of biographies of noteworthy ancient Greek and Roman statesmen and military leaders. Frequently, Plutarch compares a famous Greek to a famous Roman, pointing out similarities in personality and achievements. These expertly constructed and very readable tracts provided later historians and others, including playwrights like Shakespeare, with priceless information about prominent ancient personages and also inspired new generations of writers to tackle the multiple biography genre.

The Lucent History Makers series proudly carries on the venerable tradition handed down from Plutarch. Each volume in the series consists of a set of five to eight biographies of important and influential historical figures who were linked together by a common factor. In *Rulers of Ancient Rome*, for example, all the figures were generals, consuls, or emperors of either the Roman Republic or Empire; while the subjects of *Fighters Against American Slavery*, though they lived in different places and times, all shared the same goal, namely the eradication of human servitude. Mindful that politicians and military leaders are not (and never have been) the only people who shape the course of history, the editors of the series have also included representatives from a wide range of endeavors, including scientists, artists, writers, philosophers, religious leaders, and sports figures.

Each book is intended to give a range of figures—some well known, others less known; some who made a great impact on history, others who made only a small impact. For instance, by making Columbus's initial voyage possible, Spain's Queen Isabella I, featured in *Women Leaders of Nations*, helped to open up the New World to exploration and exploitation by the European powers. Inarguably, therefore, she made a major contribution to a series of events that had momentous consequences for the entire world. By contrast, Catherine II, the eighteenth-century Russian queen, and Golda Meir, the modern Israeli prime minister, did not play roles of global impact; however, their policies and actions significantly influenced the historical development of both their own countries and their regional neighbors. Regardless of their relative importance in the greater historical scheme, all of the figures chronicled in the History Makers series made contributions to posterity; and their public achievements, as well as what is known about their private lives, are presented and evaluated in light of the most recent scholarship.

In addition, each volume in the series is documented and substantiated by a wide array of primary and secondary source quotations. The primary source quotes enliven the text by presenting eyewitness views of the times and culture in which each history maker lived; while the secondary source quotes, taken from the works of respected modern scholars, offer expert elaboration and/ or critical commentary. Each quote is footnoted, demonstrating to the reader exactly where biographers find their information. The footnotes also provide the reader with the means of conducting additional research. Finally, to further guide and illuminate readers, each volume in the series features photographs, two bibliographies, and a comprehensive index.

The History Makers series provides both students engaged in research and more casual readers with informative, enlightening, and entertaining overviews of individuals from a variety of circumstances, professions, and backgrounds. No doubt all of them, whether loved or hated, benevolent or cruel, constructive or destructive, will remain endlessly fascinating to each new generation seeking to identify the forces that shaped their world.

"Yes, My Fuehrer"

"Hitler Dead in Chancellery, Nazis Say,"[1] screamed the headline of the *New York Times* on Wednesday, May 2, 1945. Adolf Hitler, the man whose name history would associate with the darkest days of the twentieth century, had committed suicide. In an underground bunker, sixty feet below the chancellery building that housed the German government, amid the echoes of Allied bombs falling in and around Berlin, Germany's Fuehrer, supreme leader, had put a gun to his head and killed himself.

Hitler's desire for power began in 1905, when, at age sixteen, he told his friend August Kubizek that he was destined to be a leader and spoke of "a mandate he would one day receive from the people, to lead them out of servitude to the heights of freedom."[2] At the age of thirty-one, Hitler became the head of the National Socialist German Workers' Party (*National Sozialistische Deutsche Arbeiter Partei,* also known as the NSDAP or Nazi Party), and by the time he was thirty-four, he had served a prison term for attempting to overthrow the government of Bavaria, the second largest state in Germany. When he was appointed chancellor (prime minister) of Germany on January 30, 1933, the uneducated and unrefined native of Austria had been a German citizen a mere one year.

Few German statesmen would have had the resolve or determination to lead a political party barely five years after the country's disastrous defeat in World War I. The twin humiliations of loss on the battlefield and crushing financial reparations imposed by the victors had plunged postwar Germany into economic, social, and political chaos. Inflation and unemployment were rampant. Political parties sprang up overnight, and fighting among them led to daily bloodshed. The German people wanted and needed a strong leader, a fuehrer, who could restore their country to its former place as an influential world power.

The time was ripe for Hitler, who blamed Jews and Communists for all of Germany's woes. He promised to build a reich, or empire, that would last a thousand years. Hitler envisioned a "master race" of people he described as Aryans—non-Jewish Caucasians of Nordic ancestry—to whom people of all other nationalities would be subjected. In pursuit of this dream, neighboring countries were attacked and sometimes conquered, "inferior breeds" of peoples were targeted for extermination, and the security of the entire world was threatened. Yet for reasons that are still debated, the German populace, with very few exceptions, blindly went along with Hitler's radical programs. The result led not to Germany's glory but to its downfall. In the process, 55 million people lost their lives.

The Seducer of a Nation

A good leader is one who rules a country with the best interests of its citizens in mind, vigorously encouraging cooperation in the

Adolf Hitler poses with members of the SS police force who enforced the brutality of Hitler's Third Reich.

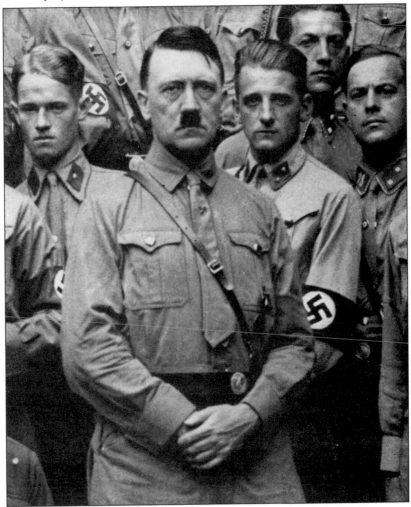

pursuit of common goals. Good leaders do not deprive their people of civil rights or rule by terror or threats. There are checks and balances under good leadership and the opportunity to correct mistakes. A country becomes "better" under a good ruler—more economically, intellectually, and culturally prosperous. Good leaders work toward unification and strive to bring it about within the borders of their own country as well as with their neighbors. Good leaders protect the people under their authority.

Hitler seduced a nation with charisma, but he was a good leader only on the most superficial level. He had one way of doing things: his way. To assist him with the implementation of the policies of his Nazi government, Hitler surrounded himself with henchmen—devotees whose only purpose in life was to serve Adolf Hitler. Hitler did not desire to have around him "clever" people who had thoughts of their own; rather, Hitler preferred those who would act on the thoughts that he put into their heads. To build Nazi Germany, therefore, Hitler chose henchmen who lived for his approval, and these powerful men responded to every command he uttered with blind obedience: "Yes, my Fuehrer."

Hitler had four requirements for his henchmen. They had to champion a "master race"; condemn those Hitler condemned; further the causes of Hitler's political philosophy, national socialism, by adhering to its precepts; and adore Adolf Hitler. "When one enters the Reich Chancellery, one should have the feeling that he is visiting the master of the world,"[3] Hitler once said of himself. Hitler selected followers who, for various reasons, needed to idolize a human being, and he exploited their needs expertly. Hitler's followers claimed to be ready to die for him, and, in the end, several did—either by their own hand or on the gallows at Nuremberg for having committed crimes against humanity during World War II.

Many of Hitler's henchmen had the same beliefs he did. They also had needs for approval, love, and affection. Most were ambitious and eager to share in the Fuehrer's fame and power. As siblings compete for the love and attention of a parent, each wanted to be "Hitler's favorite." Hitler's closest henchmen disliked one another and were jealous of Hitler's relationships with their peers. Hitler encouraged jealousy and competition among his henchmen. It assured him that they would not join forces and become stronger than he was.

William L. Shirer says of Hitler's henchmen in his book *The Rise and Fall of the Third Reich: A History of Nazi Germany,*

Hitler (second from right) stands with other Nazi officials at a congressional meeting.

In a normal society they surely would have stood out as a grotesque assortment of misfits. But in the last chaotic days of the Republic, they began to appear to millions of befuddled Germans as saviors. . . . They were led by a man who knew exactly what he wanted and they were ruthless enough, and opportunist enough, to go to any lengths to help him get it.[4]

The sheer size of the Third Reich, as it expanded beyond Germany's borders, required thousands of henchmen to implement Nazi government policies on a daily basis. Hitler's favorites were bestowed with positions of authority requiring the utmost loyalty and obedience. Five of them are profiled in this book. Hermann Goering, the commander of the Luftwaffe, the German air force, was a morphine addict who was Hitler's chosen successor. Dr. Joseph Goebbels had an inferiority complex stemming from a childhood deformity. The lies he publicized as Hitler's minister for propaganda and public enlightenment persuaded the German populace to accept Hitler's policies and did much to conceal from the rest of the world the horrors of Nazi Germany. Heinrich Himmler, the chief of Hitler's autonomous political police force, the Gestapo, was responsible for the deaths of millions. Rudolf

Hess was Hitler's deputy; despite his adoration of Hitler, the Fuehrer would denounce him as insane. Baldur von Schirach was in charge of Hitler's next generation of Nazis. He implemented and organized the exploitive Hitler Youth program.

Hitler's henchmen knew that their devotion to their Fuehrer would forever link their names to his, but even they were not sure how future generations would see them. As Goebbels said shortly before his death, "We shall go down in history as the greatest statesmen of all time, or as the greatest criminals."[5]

CHAPTER 1

The Third Reich of a Thousand Years

By late 1918, General Paul von Hindenburg and his chief of staff, Erich Ludendorff, leaders of the overwhelmed German army, realized that their country would not be victorious in World War I and approached the Allies with a request for peace. The United States, Great Britain, and France refused to negotiate with Germany unless a democratic government was established. On November 10, 1918, Kaiser Wilhelm II abdicated to Holland, and on November 11, in a railroad dining car in the Compiegne Forest in northern France, a

A jubilant President Woodrow Wilson (center) leads a procession commemorating the 1919 Treaty of Versailles. The signing of the treaty ended World War I.

delegation from Germany headed by Matthias Erzberger surrendered to the Allies, ending World War I. Soon after, a German national assembly met in the city of Weimar to write a new constitution transforming the German empire into a democratic republic. The new regime headed by socialists Friedrich Ebert and Phillip Scheidemann became known as the Weimar Republic. In June 1919, the representatives of the Weimar Republic reluctantly signed the Treaty of Versailles, hence accepting punitive terms.

The treaty, reflective of the fact that Germany had been the principal aggressor in the war, brought the country to its knees. For example, the treaty required Germany to surrender its overseas colonies and forfeit land to Belgium, Czechoslovakia, Denmark, and France. The new boundaries meant that large numbers of German citizens no longer lived in Germany. In addition, Germany was fined billions of deutsche marks in war reparations and had to agree to give France control of its coalfields and permit the Allied occupation of the west bank of the Rhine River. Germany was also forbidden to build an army exceeding 100,000 soldiers, was allowed only a small navy, and had to abolish what remained of its air force and agree not to rebuild it.

A 1915 photograph shows a young Hitler in the Kaiser's Imperial Army regalia.

The Weimar Republic emphasized a centralized national government over the independence of individual German states. It called for a president, elected by an assembly, who could appoint a chancellor to help with the running of the government. Because the Weimar Republic had agreed to the Treaty of Versailles, the new government was not generally accepted by the German people. The consensus was that the Weimar leaders, many of whom were Marxist Jews, were traitors who had stabbed Germany in the back. One of the Weimar Republic's most vocal critics was Adolf Hitler. Although he was born in Austria, Hitler considered himself a German. He had served as a corporal in the Kaiser's Imperial Army during the war and had been twice decorated with the Iron Cross for bravery. Hitler shared the outrage of the German people regarding the terms of surrender. He called the leaders of the Weimar Republic the "November criminals" and blamed them for the abdication of the kaiser, Germany's defeat in World War I, and the acceptance of the punishing terms at Versailles.

New German Nationalism

In 1919, before being mustered out of the German army stationed in Munich, Hitler attended a meeting of the German Workers' Party. A nationalist working-class group, the party endorsed the need for a strong anti-Communist Germany. Hitler joined the party and was soon captivating audiences as its "advertising chairman." Albert Speer, an architect who was to become one of Hitler's Reich ministers, explains Hitler's charisma: "I was . . . becoming a follower of Hitler, whose magnetic force had reached out to me the first time I saw him. . . . His persuasiveness, the peculiar magic of his by no means pleasant voice, the oddity of his rather banal manner . . . all that bewildered and fascinated me."[6]

Hitler was instrumental in developing the "twenty-five points" that were to become the foundation of the German Workers' Party. By 1922, Hitler had taken control of the group and changed its name to the National Socialist German Workers' Party, soon shortened to Nazi. Hitler objected to the way the Weimar Marxists favored class distinction and encouraged labor unions. He wanted the German people to consider themselves Germans foremost and members of a class second. He did not want to see workers unite; he wanted to see all Germans unite.

The Nazi Party was built on three main precepts: Germany's troubles were caused by the Marxist Jews known as the "November criminals," the Treaty of Versailles should be rescinded, and Jews should no longer be allowed to be German citizens. Hitler had a particular hatred of Jews; he believed they were involved in an international conspiracy to rule the world. Hitler gave rousing speeches that brought in new party members by the thousands. As a result, the Nazi Party also became known as the "Hitler movement." Germans demonstrated their respect for Hitler by hailing him like a Roman emperor, shouting, "Heil Hitler!" and raising their right arms in a forty-five-degree-angle salute, a gesture that would become the standard greeting throughout Nazi Germany.

The Nazis

To reinforce the Nazis' new image, Hitler designed a banner using red, white, and black—the colors of Germany under the kaiser. The

An SA storm trooper waves the Nazi flag above a German valley in this propagandistic postcard.

red background symbolized the party's socialism, while the white disc in the center stood for the party's nationalist position. The black hooked cross, the swastika, displayed on the white disc represented the conflict for Aryan victory. The Nazi banner became a symbol of the group's anti-Semitism. Hitler also believed that the Nazis should have their own army, and he put Ernst Roehm, one of the originators of the Nazi Party, in charge of *Sturmabteilung*, or SA, known in English as the storm troopers. Many of the storm troopers were World War I veterans who proudly wore swastika armbands over their brown uniform shirts, but many others were vagrants and drifters. Hitler did not mind who joined the SA as long as they were "only those who want to be obedient to the *fuehrer* and are prepared to die if necessary!"[7] The storm troopers roamed the streets of Munich looking for opportunities to attack Communists and Jews.

In 1925, another police force, the *Schutzstaffel,* or SS or shock troops, formed under the SA. Eventually, the SS became the elite group of soldiers that served as Hitler's private bodyguards. They wore black uniforms with a death's-head insignia and took an oath to protect Hitler from everyone, including the SA. Soon, yet another internal security agency was formed, the secret state police (*Geheime Staatspolizei*), the terror-inspiring Gestapo.

With the Nazi Party behind him and a strong police presence to support him, Hitler espoused the slogan "Today Germany; Tomorrow the World!"[8] and planned a revolt to take over the government.

The Beer Hall Putsch

The German people desperately wanted a strong leader who would restore Germany to its prewar greatness. Arrogantly assuming that he was such a man, on November 8, 1923, Hitler, along with some of his followers, attempted a government takeover in the Burgerbrauhaus, a popular beer hall located on the outskirts of the Bavarian city of Munich. In the debacle, referred to as the "Beer Hall Putsch" (coup), Hitler arrested the highest Bavarian commissar, the general in charge of the German army in Bavaria, and the head of

The SA raise the swastika flag during the Beer Hall Putsch, Hitler's 1923 government takeover.

the state. Owing largely to a combination of ineptness and bad planning, however, Hitler was unable to accomplish his goal of forming a provisional German national government.

The coup was crushed by the police as its participants marched down the streets of Munich. Hitler was convicted of high treason and was sentenced to five years in Bavaria's Landsberg Prison. The Nazi Party and SA were banned, and the Nazi treasury was confiscated by the government. Hitler served less than one year of his sentence. While imprisoned, he began writing his autobiography, *Mein Kampf* (My Struggle), the book that came to be known as the Nazi Bible. An admirer named Rudolf Hess, who had participated in the putsch and had also been jailed, helped Hitler write the book.

Hitler reads a newspaper while serving a sentence for treason after the failure of the putsch.

During Hitler's imprisonment, the banned Nazi Party had dwindled to seven hundred members, having lost importance as Americans helped to ease Germany's inflation by investing in its factories. Upon his release from prison, Hitler took advantage of the temporary prosperity to rebuild the Nazi Party. When the U.S. stock market crashed in 1929, sparking a worldwide depression, the demand for German-made products fell. By the end of 1931, 5.6 million Germans were unemployed, and Hitler was once again emerging as a promising savior.

The Death of German Democracy

Having experienced tremendous growth after 1929, the Nazi Party swept the elections of July 27, 1932, becoming the strongest party in the Reichstag (Germany's elected legislature). On January 30, 1933, against his better judgment, President Paul von Hindenburg appointed Hitler chancellor (prime minister) of Germany, the second most powerful position in the country. Hermann Goering became president of the Reichstag, and Dr. Joseph Goebbels was made director of the Bureau of Propaganda.

One month after Hitler's appointment, there was a fire in the building in which the Reichstag meetings were held. Hitler accused the Communists of arson and over the next few days ordered the arrest and imprisonment of four thousand Communist Party members. A vagrant eventually admitted to setting the Reichstag fire, but Hitler nevertheless was able to use the incident to persuade President Hindenburg to sign a decree "for the Protection of the People and the State." The law suspended several civil liberties, including freedom of the press. Mail was censored, and people were searched and arrested for any or no reason.

In March 1933, the German people went to the polls to elect members of the Reichstag. It was to be the last democratic election under Hitler. Immediately after the February 27, 1933, Reichstag fire, Hitler moved one step closer to taking total control of Germany when he proposed the dissolution of the Reichstag. This measure, the Enabling Act, needed the approval of the Reichstag, but the Nazis did not have enough votes. "The answer is simple," said Reichstag president Goering. "We will arrest all the Communist deputies and enough Social Democrats to frighten the rest, and then we will put the Enabling Act to the vote."[9]

The Birth of the Third Reich

Hitler had come to power legally, but in the process German democracy had been killed. Hitler referred to his dictatorship as the

"Third Reich." Germany's First Reich had been the Holy Roman Empire, which began with Charlemagne in 800 and lasted until 1806. The Second Reich was ruled by Otto von Bismarck, a Prussian whose influence made Germany Europe's most powerful nation from 1871 to 1918. Hitler claimed that his Third Reich would last one thousand years.

As soon as Hitler gained control of the government, he dissolved all labor unions and had their leaders killed, beaten, or imprisoned. All political parties except the Nazis were banned, and only Nazis could hold government positions. Jewish businesses were confiscated and turned over to non-Jews. Thousands of books written by authors who espoused anti-Nazi doctrine were burned in huge bonfires. Freedom of the press was further restricted; newspapers and radio could only report the information given to them by the Department of Propaganda. Movies had to be prescreened before they could be shown in German cinemas. A national Reich church was established.

Hitler became judge, jury, and executioner. "If anyone reproaches me and asks why I did not resort to the regular courts of justice, then all I can say is . . . in this hour I was responsible for the fate of the German people, and thereby I became the supreme judge," [10] he explained. His ruthlessness even extended to members of his own party. By 1934, the SA had grown to formidable numbers, and mem-

German citizens congregate around a truckload of anti-Nazi books to be burned by the Nazis.

bers of the organization wanted to be recognized for their contributions to the Nazi Party. SA leaders planned a "second revolution"—to overthrow and kill Hitler and other high-ranking Nazis. Goering and Goebbels became aware of the plot, however, and knowing that such a disruption might cause President Hindenburg to outlaw the Nazi Party and declare martial law, they persuaded Hitler to conduct a "blood purge" of the SA. On the night of June 30, 1934, which would later be known as the Night of the Long Knives, hundreds of SA members in Berlin and Munich, including Roehm, were apprehended by the SS and executed.

President Hindenburg died approximately one month later. Within one hour of his death, Hitler combined the offices of Germany's president and chancellor and appointed himself to the new position. The German economy flourished as Hitler put people to work manufacturing munitions, an activity the drafters of the Treaty of Versailles had hoped to forestall. Hitler instituted a "Strength Through Joy" program that rewarded laborers with vacations, theater tickets, and other bonuses. Many ordinary citizens, however, felt Hitler was not good for Germany. Klaus P. Fischer says in his book *Nazi Germany*, "Although thousands of Germans cheered [Hitler's] triumph . . . the record also shows that many Germans of all walks of life were gripped by fear and apprehension, strongly suspecting that Hitler would unleash a flood of sewage all over Germany and the world at large."[11]

The Birth of the Holocaust

Hitler's anti-Semitic views most likely originated when he was a struggling artist living in Vienna. "I have joined the Anti-Semitic League and I have also put your name down,"[12] Hitler told his friend August Kubizek around 1910. The German Workers' Party, and later the Nazi Party, offered Hitler contact with others who shared his views and were willing to act on their feelings. By the time he wrote *Mein Kampf* in 1924, Hitler was portraying Jews as "maggots in a rotting corpse, germ carriers, vampires sucking the blood of others, and spreaders of syphilis."[13] Hitler blamed the Jews for all of society's ills. He saw the Jewish people not as adherents of a religion but as a race, which he planned to dominate. He envisioned the formation of a "master Aryan race" to accomplish this.

When Hitler became chancellor in 1933, there were 550,000 Jews in Germany, which represented 1 percent of the population. Immediately after coming to power, the Nazi regime began implementing programs of Jewish persecution. Hitler was formulating

An anti-Semitic sign supports the German boycott of Jewish businesses.

a "Final Solution" to the "Jewish Problem." Jewish businesses were boycotted. Jews were forbidden to hold public office and to attend public schools and universities.

The September 1935 Nuremberg Laws made German Jews second-class citizens. Among other restrictions, Jews were no longer allowed to marry non-Jews. In 1937, all Jewish men were required to use the middle name "Israel" on their identification cards, and women were required to use "Sarah." This was followed by a succession of rules barring Jews from going to public places, owning businesses, and walking on the streets during Nazi holidays, culminating in a ruling in September 1941 that all Jews over the age of six must wear a yellow Star of David badge on their outer clothing. To Hitler, the Jews were *untermenschen,* "undesirables," who, if they were unable to serve the Aryans as slaves, must die.

By the late 1930s, all unemployed Jews were required to work. In an attempt to make Germany "Jew free," Jewish families were forced from their homes and made to live in overcrowded ghettos outside of Germany. Several families shared the living space designed for one family. Food was scarce and hundreds of people perished daily from exposure, starvation, and disease.

By the early 1940s, deportation by train to "work camps" in the east was under way. In reality, Jews were being transferred to forced labor and concentration camps. The camps, based on a model used by the British during the Boer War, had been set up in the early days of the Nazi regime. They were originally designed to incarcerate political prisoners for "reeducation" in Nazi doctrine, but they soon became a means of terror and death—not only for Jews but for all of Hitler's *untermenschen,* including Poles, Gypsies, the handicapped, the mentally ill, and homosexuals.

A Jewish couple wear yellow Star of David badges in accordance with Nazi law.

Kristallnacht

In November 1938, a young Pole named Hershel Grynszpan, distraught over his father's imprisonment in a concentration camp, killed an official at the German embassy in Paris. On the evening of November 9, 1938, in what appeared to be spontaneous acts of revenge but was actually a Nazi directive inspired by a speech by Goebbels, the SA, SS, and frenzied mobs of Nazi sympathizers retaliated by breaking the windows of Jewish homes and businesses throughout Germany and Austria (which had been annexed to Germany earlier that same year). Synagogues were desecrated and burned, and Jews were assaulted in their homes. More than ninety Jews were killed, either executed or attacked as they defended their property and synagogues. Thirty thousand Jewish men were sent to concentration camps. November 9, 1938, became known as *Kristallnacht*, the "Night of Broken Glass." It marked the beginning of an accelerated program of anti-Semitic terror by the Nazis.

The Road to World War II

Beginning in 1933, first covertly and then in open violation of the Treaty of Versailles, Germany had been building a military machine of modern tanks and armored cars. Hitler had also been rebuilding an air force, and his army numbered more than 1 million troops. He was planning to invade neighboring countries to acquire *Lebensraum* (living space) for his "master Aryan race." Hitler tested the Treaty of Versailles in 1936 by sending troops into the demilitarized Rhineland. Fearful of starting another world war, France did not strike back. Meeting no resistance from France, Hitler threatened to take German-speaking Austria by force if the Austrian leaders did not peacefully sign an agreement allowing Hitler to occupy their country. The German word *Anschluss* is used to describe the resulting annexation of Austria to Germany.

Hitler's next target was the Sudetenland, eleven thousand square miles of Czechoslovakia, rich in natural resources and populated by many German-speaking people. The Czech army and the French army together vastly outnumbered the Germans, and historians today believe that World War II could have been averted if the Czechs had resisted. This did not happen, however, and in an act of diplomatic capitulation, other European countries, without consulting Czechoslovakia, agreed that Germany could occupy the Sudetenland as well as half of Czechoslovakia. The Germans promptly seized the other half.

Without German bloodshed, Hitler had added over 10 million people and two countries to his Reich, but even he was aware that there would eventually be resistance to his invasions. "Further success can no longer be attained without the shedding of blood,"[14] he told his leaders as he prepared a strategy to take over Poland. "There is no question . . . we are left with the decision to attack Poland at the first suitable opportunity,"[15] Hitler said in May 1939.

World War II Begins

Anticipating French and British retaliation for his planned invasion of Poland, Hitler believed he needed Russian leader Joseph Stalin's support for the incursion. In August 1939, Germany and Russia signed a ten-year Nazi-Soviet nonaggression pact in which the two countries agreed not to attack each other and to share in the conquest of Poland. Few had been surprised when in 1936, Hitler formed an alliance with Benito Mussolini, the fascist dictator of Italy, but the pact with Stalin was an about-face for Hitler, who had condemned Communists for much of his life.

On September 1, 1939, the Germans dressed concentration camp prisoners in Polish uniforms and forced them to attack a German radio station. When news of the incident became public, Hitler said he had no choice "except to meet force with force."[16] He retaliated with military strikes on land with tanks and by air with fighter aircraft. Two days later, England and France declared war on Germany, beginning World War II.

By June 1940, most of the countries in Europe, including France, had been occupied by the Germans. Every conquered country added additional troops to the German army. In September 1940, General Hideki Tojo of Japan joined Mussolini and Hitler in a "Pact of Steel." England, fortified with American tanks, ammunition, guns, and food, was fighting the Axis Powers on its own on two fronts—in Europe and North Africa. Hitler anxiously awaited a surrender from British prime minister Winston Churchill, but England endured wave after wave of bombings by the German air force, the Luftwaffe.

In June 1941, Germany broke its nonaggression pact and invaded Russia. Shivering in their summer uniforms, the Germans were unprepared for the Russian winter with its temperatures of ten degrees above zero. They retreated from well-provisioned Russian troops who blocked their attempt to take Moscow during the winter of 1941–1942. In November 1942, Stalingrad fell to the Germans. Within days, the Russians began a counteroffensive and trapped 250,000 German troops in the city. Hitler forbade the Germans to surrender and ordered them to fight to the last man and the last round of ammunition. It would be two months before the starved, exhausted, and frostbitten Germans capitulated. By then, their numbers had dwindled to 91,000. Stalingrad was Germany's worst defeat.

On June 6, 1944, D day, the Allies, fortified with American troops, invaded the Normandy coast to begin the liberation of France, and in late December of the same year, they won a decisive victory at Bastogne, Belgium. A few days later, the Russian army broke through the Polish front and headed toward Berlin.

Hitler's Last Days

By the time the Russians entered Germany, Hitler was a broken man. Since 1941, his physical and mental health had deteriorated. He complained of weakness, chills, and insomnia, and he could not control the shaking of his left arm and leg. Walking and maintaining his balance became difficult. Hitler had also become addicted to drugs containing the poison strychnine that were given to him

World War II 1943–1945

Axis occupation
Allied nations
Neutral nations
Major Allied drives
Major battles

Murmansk
Norwegian Sea
Narvik
Trondheim
FINLAND
Gulf of Bothnia
Leningrad
North Atlantic Ocean
NORWAY
SWEDEN
Oslo
Stockholm
USSR
Moscow
North Sea
DENMARK
Hamburg
Baltic Sea
IRELAND
GREAT BRITAIN
London
NETHERLANDS
Antwerp
BELGIUM
Berlin
Warsaw
Kursk July 1943
Kiev
Stalingrad
English Channel
Normandy Invasion June 6, 1944
Battle of the Bulge Dec. 1944
GERMANY
Paris
FRANCE
SWITZERLAND
Vienna
SLOVAKIA
HUNGARY
Budapest
ROMANIA
Bay of Biscay
Rhone Valley Invasion
ITALY
YUGOSLAVIA
Black Sea
IRAN
PORTUGAL
SPAIN
Madrid
Rome
Adriatic Sea
Cassino Nov. 1943
Anzio Jan. 1944
Salerno Sept. 1943
ALBANIA
BULGARIA
GREECE
Aegean Sea
TURKEY
Mediterranean Sea
Ionian Sea
Athens
CYPRUS
SYRIA
Algiers
Tunis
SICILY
Sicily Invaded July-August 1943
CRETE
LEBANON
IRAQ
Casablanca
Oran
ALGERIA
MOROCCO
Kasserine Pass Feb. 1943
TUNISIA
Tripoli
Benghazi
PALESTINE
TRANS-JORDAN
Cairo
SAUDI ARABIA
LIBYA
EGYPT

Scale of Miles
500

by his doctor to calm his nerves. As the Allied forces headed toward Berlin, Hitler blamed his generals for Germany's defeat and retreated to his bunker under the chancellery building. At times, he was out of touch with reality and ordered the amassing of troops that had been lost to the Russians the previous year. With the Russian army across the street from the chancellery, Hitler and his wife, Eva Braun, whom he had married a few hours prior, took their lives. At their request, the bodies were burned in the garden. It is believed that the relentless Russian shelling of the chancellery complex obliterated all traces of their incinerated remains.

On the evening of May 1, 1945, Hamburg radio put the German people on standby for an important announcement. No indication as to the message of the broadcast was given. At 9:40 P.M., the slow movement from Bruckner's Seventh Symphony was played over the airwaves. Then came the news: Adolf Hitler, Fuehrer of Germany, was dead. The Nazi reign of Germany, which Hitler had claimed would last one thousand years, had lasted a mere 147 months.

CHAPTER 2

Hermann Goering

The main streets of Berlin were awash with torchlight the evening of January 30, 1933. Hundreds of thousands of Nazi supporters filled the streets, waving small swastika flags and cheering as the brown-shirted SA police force marched by. The parade moved down the Wilhelmstrasse and passed the chancellery where Hitler stood at a window surveying the procession. The people of Berlin were celebrating an announcement made earlier in the day by Germany's president, Paul von Hindenburg. Hitler had been named chancellor of the German Reich.

Over and over again, Hitler raised his arm and acknowledged the crowds with the Nazi salute. Standing beside him, Hermann Goering, the president of the Reichstag and future Reich marshall, was broadcasting a message to the people of Germany:

> My German comrades . . . January 30, 1933, will enter Germany's history as the day on which the nation, after fourteen

Hitler stands (eighth from left) with cabinet members of the new German Reich.

Hitler sits beside Hermann Goering, second-in-command of the Third Reich.

years of anguish, pain, and shame, is restored to its former glory. . . . The young new *Fuehrer* . . . will lead the nation to a new and better future. . . . May the German people herald this day . . . inspired by the new faith [that] the future will bring us what we have fought for . . . bread and work for the German people, freedom and honor for the nation.[17]

Goering beamed with self-satisfaction. As leader of the Reichstag, he had worked tirelessly for a year to persuade President Hindenburg to name Hitler chancellor of the German Reich. Goering had sworn an oath of allegiance to Hitler upon first meeting him twelve years earlier, and his determination to see Hitler named chancellor was an expression of his loyalty.

Goering was a patriotic man, but he also had an insatiable appetite for power. He saw in Hitler the promise of a reborn Germany, a powerful country that would first rule Europe and then the world. Goering's lust for power would ultimately cause the terrorization and death of millions of people in Nazi Germany. As Hitler's second-in-command, Goering would be responsible for the creation of the Gestapo, the building of concentration camps, and the persecution of the Jews. The German air force, the Luftwaffe, also under Goering, would extend Nazi terror to other European countries.

"A View Few Other Men Will Ever See"

Hermann Goering was born on January 12, 1893, in the small German town of Rosenheim, forty miles south of Munich. Goering's mother, Franziska, was twenty-seven years old when she gave birth to him, her fourth child and second son. Goering's father, Heinrich Ernst Goering, a senior official in Germany's consular service, was twenty-five years older than Franziska. Franziska christened her new son Hermann Wilhelm Goering, naming him after Hermann von Epenstein, a doctor and friend of the family who bore the title "Ritter," identifying him as a member of the minor nobility. Goering's middle name, Wilhelm, was in honor of Kaiser Wilhelm II.

Heinrich Goering's government position relocated him and his growing family outside of Germany. When Hermann Goering was three months old, his mother left him in Bavaria to join her husband and older children in Haiti, where the elder Goering served as consul general. During the first three years of his life, Goering was raised by a couple with two young daughters. His loneliness for his real parents was expressed in his temperamental behavior toward his foster parents. "It is the cruelest thing that can happen to a child, to be torn from his mother in his formative years,"[18] Goering said as an adult about the years without Franziska.

Returning to Germany in 1896, Heinrich settled his family in a suburb of Berlin. Continually passed over for advancement, he turned to alcohol to ease the disappointment in his career. As a child, Goering was close to his mother, but his relationship with his father was strained. It was Epenstein who became a father figure to him. He was wealthy, well traveled, and well placed in society. Around the turn of the century, Epenstein invited the Goering family to live in his castle at Mauterndorf in Austria. Franziska and her host entered into a romantic relationship that resulted in the birth of Goering's younger brother, Albert, when Goering was seven years old.

At Mauterndorf, Goering was able to indulge in a favorite childhood game, the imaginary reenactment of medieval battles. He was a stubborn child who insisted on being the leader when playing games. Goering became skilled at mountain climbing when he was ten years old. "I have no fear of heights," he said. "They stimulate me. Besides, any danger is worth while if, by risking it, you reach the top of the mountain. You know you will have a view few other men will ever see."[19]

These words, spoken at a young age, were an early indication of Goering's outlook on life. Ambition seemed to be a dominant part of his personality even as a youngster, and, like his father and Epenstein, both old cavalry men, Goering wanted to enter the military.

"I was bored with school, all I wanted to be was a soldier,"[20] he said in recalling his decision to leave boarding school without consulting his parents. After returning home, Goering was enrolled in a military academy at Karlsruhe. When he graduated at age sixteen, his report read, "He has developed a quality that should take him far: he is not afraid to take a risk."[21]

After Karlsruhe, Goering entered Lichterfeld, a college for future German army officers. Graduating with high honors in 1912, Goering accepted a commission as a lieutenant in the 112th Prince Wilhelm Infantry Regiment. His unit was headquartered in Mulhausen, located in Alsace-Lorraine, part of the territory annexed from France after the war of 1870. When France declared war on Germany in 1914, Goering's troops were forced to cross the Rhine River in retreat.

An Ace Pilot to the End

Back in Germany, Goering became reacquainted with fellow officer Bruno Loerzer, an old friend from Mulhausen. Loerzer was training to be a pilot in the fledgling German air force. Goering found the idea of fighting the war in the air more appealing than fighting in the trenches along the western front. Using Epenstein's influence, Goering obtained a place in an air force unit as a reconnaissance flight photographer. While Loerzer piloted the small single-engine plane, Goering photographed the French battlefields, gripping the sides of the cockpit with his feet and legs as he hung out over the side of the plane. This earned him the nickname the "Flying Trapezist."

Goering soon tired of photography. He longed to serve Germany as a pilot and began training at Freiburg in June 1915. Upon completion of the three-month course, Goering was commissioned to a convoy of twin-engine fighter planes. He had been flying for only three weeks when his plane

Prior to his Nazi career, Goering served as a German lieutenant in World War I.

29

was fired upon and badly damaged by a British Handley-Page bomber. Goering was injured when he crash-landed in German territory, and he spent several months on medical leave. In 1918, at the age of twenty-five, Goering was given command of the squadron that had been headed by Baron Manfred von Richthofen, the "Red Baron" who had been shot down by the Royal Air Force.

As the leader of Richthofen's old unit, Goering was very successful, downing twenty-two enemy planes. He was awarded Germany's highest honor, the Iron Cross, among many other distinguished awards, and returned home a national hero.

World War I ended in defeat for Germany, however, and Goering was ordered to ground his planes and surrender to the approaching Allies. He assembled his men together and made this announcement: "They are orders I do not propose to obey! I will allow neither my men nor my machines to fall into the hands of the enemy. We cannot stay here and fight on. But we can make sure that when the end comes, we will be in Germany. . . . As for our planes, we will fly them out—to Darmstadt."[22] Only a partial squadron returned to Darmstadt by air, and upon landing, on Goering's orders, the planes were smashed beyond repair. Even with the fragile armistice at risk, Goering indulged his penchant for having his own way.

An able fighter pilot during World War I, Goering later returned home a national hero.

Postwar Disillusions

In 1919, Goering went to live with his widowed mother in Munich. Postwar Munich was beset by violence, as German citizens, their savings wiped out by economic inflation and facing deprivation and starvation, took to the streets in protest. Goering became disillusioned with his beloved Germany, while mourning its defeat, and he resented the hardships caused by its surrender.

Like many of his fellow countrymen, Goering was unemployed. Piloting an airplane was his only skill, but commercial aviation was still in the future. Germany had been forbidden to have an air force by the Treaty of Versailles, so a military career as a pilot was not an option. Goering managed to eke out a living offering sightseeing tours by air and operating an air taxi to Scandinavia. Depressed and uncertain of his future, he enrolled in and dropped out of the University of Munich. His primary preoccupation during the postwar years was searching for a political means of restoring his country to its prewar glory.

There was, however, one bright light in Goering's disappointment and depression. He met and fell in love with Carin von Kantzow, a Swedish baroness who was thirty-two years old, married, and the mother of an eight-year-old son. Kantzow returned the affections of the dashing war hero, and after obtaining an amicable divorce from her baron husband, she and Goering were married on February 3, 1923.

An Early Hitler Supporter

Goering's first encounter with the man who was to become Germany's Fuehrer was in November 1922 at one of Munich's many Nazi meetings to protest the Treaty of Versailles. Goering found in Hitler and his National Socialist German Workers' Party the political and social agenda for which he had been searching. He said of that first meeting with Hitler: "The convictions [of Hitler] were spoken word for word as if from my own soul. Now, finally I saw a man that had clear and definite aims. I just wanted to speak to him . . . and see if I could assist him in any way. He received me at once and after I had introduced myself, he said it was an extraordinary turn of fate that we should meet."[23]

The two men shared opinions about the unfairness of the Treaty of Versailles and the betrayal of those Germans, mainly Jews and Marxists, whose acquiescence to the Allies caused Germany to lose the war. Hitler and Goering became close political allies, and Goering vowed his complete support to Hitler. Goering and his wife, Carin, who had also completely embraced the Nazi Party, often

Hitler assigned Goering to reorganize the SA (pictured here marching) after learning of his impressive military record.

hosted Nazi meetings at their new home in Obermenzing. Impressed with the pilot's war record, Hitler immediately assigned him to reorganize the brown-shirted *Sturmabteilung* (SA), a private army now numbering eleven thousand men.

Thus, Goering was at the head of the steel-helmeted storm troopers the night Hitler attempted to overthrow the Bavarian government in the Beer Hall Putsch. In the early hours of the attempted coup, with the Nazi flag flying, Hitler, Goering, the SA men, and some local supporters took to the streets. The Munich police was called out, and they fired into the crowd, effectively ending the rebellion. Badly wounded by a gunshot in the thigh, Goering was arrested and given medical treatment. Hospitalized under heavy guard, he and his wife received the help of friendly policemen and disguised SA, and they were able to escape to Austria. Nazi sympathizers brought the Goerings' clothes and other possessions from Obermenzing, but the German government froze their bank account and seized their car. In unbearable pain, Goering began receiving twice-daily morphine injections for his injuries.

Political Exile and Return

The Goerings eventually wore out their welcome in Austria, and in the summer of 1925 the couple traveled to Carin's homeland of Sweden. Never one to enjoy good health, Carin began suffering from epileptic seizures in addition to continued heart and lung problems. Depressed by the failure of the Beer Hall Putsch, the constant pain of his gunshot wound, and his inability to find a job, Goering increased his self-injections of morphine to as many as six times a day. The drug caused him to experience personality changes, rages, and nervousness. The strain of Goering's addiction further aggravated Carin's health, and in September 1925, after attacking a nurse, Goering was sent to Langbro Asylum for the insane. In three months, he was morphine free and discharged.

In 1927, Germany granted amnesty to all political exiles. After being away for four years, Goering returned home to find that Hitler and his Nazi Party had increased in popularity. The years of exile gave Goering a fierce determination to work his way back into a prominent position with the Nazis. In the spring of 1928, with Hitler's blessing, Goering ran a political campaign to be elected to the Reichstag, a position he won.

Hitler once again recognized Goering's attributes—his devotion to national socialism, his status as a war hero, and his oratorical ability to persuade a crowd—and assigned him to recruit new Nazi Party members. The German people were weary of deprivation and tired of the frequent bloody conflicts that arose as different political factions fought over who would best govern Germany. Germans were easily persuaded to become Nazi sympathizers, if not downright supporters.

Goering gives a rousing speech at a Nazi rally while Hitler looks on (lower left).

From Tragedy to Triumph

Goering's bask in the glow of personal and party achievement was marred by tragedy when on October 17, 1931, his beloved wife, Carin, succumbed to tuberculosis. Although in mourning, Goering continued to campaign for the Nazis. His political speeches drew as many as forty-thousand people. As bloodshed between the different political factions continued, the people of Germany called for a new election. The results of the July 27, 1932, election gave the National Socialists 230 votes in the Reichstag, almost 100 more than the Social Democrats. Goering was elected president of the Reichstag. In his opening address, he said,

> The glorious record of the German people will always find a ready champion in me. I proclaim . . . that this session has clearly proved that the new Reichstag has a large working majority, and is capable of conducting the affairs of State without recourse to emergency measures. . . . The honor of the people, the safety of the nation and the freedom of the Fatherland will be the chief guiding stars of all my actions.[24]

On January 30, 1933, upon being appointed chancellor of Germany, Hitler immediately appointed Goering Prussian minister of the interior, a post that gave him control of the justice departments, the Prussian police, and the Gestapo, the secret police Goering founded and headed until turning it over to Heinrich Himmler in 1936.

The Third Reich

With the Nazi Party firmly in control of the German government, Hitler further promoted Goering to the position of prime minister of Prussia, and, as such, Goering set and controlled government policy. On March 1, 1935, Hitler made Goering minister of aviation. Ignoring the Treaty of Versailles ban on an air force, Goering began to amass German airpower. Thousands of young men were trained to become pilots, and thousands of Germans labored in factories producing planes and munitions. In 1937, Goering, who knew little about economics, was appointed to administer Hitler's four-year plan for economic development. The goal was to stockpile armaments for Germany's war machine. This called for major changes in the allocation of the country's resources and industrial capacity. Not long after the *Anschluss* (Germany's 1938 annexation of Austria), the production of munitions had increased 100 percent. Industries that produced goods not essential to the war were closed down. Half the consumer goods produced were given to the army. When citizens complained about the deprivation, Goering presented them with examples of his Nazi logic. "Rearmament is only a first step to make our people happy," he lectured. "We have no butter, my good people, but I ask you, would you rather have butter or guns? . . . Preparedness makes us powerful. Butter makes us fat,"[25] Goering told the German people.

As head of the Nazi Gestapo and Luftwaffe, Goering often visited his country house to alleviate stress.

A Family Man

Goering coped with the stress of being Hitler's second-in-command by overeating, and by the time he was in his early forties, he weighed 280 pounds. He periodically used saunas, exercise, and diet pills to slim down. When a neck injury forced him to seek a doctor's care, Goering once again became addicted to painkillers.

The medication helped Goering balance his life as a powerful Nazi ruler with that of a country gentleman. Goering built a large hunting lodge in Schorfheide, two hours by car from Berlin. He named his new home Carin Hall after his deceased wife. Visitors to Carin Hall were often greeted by Goering dressed in ostentatious costumes and fancy uniforms, wearing spectacular jewelry and his military medals. Upon receiving one particular visitor,

> [Goering] appeared early in a Bavarian leather jacket with full white shirt sleeves. He changed his costume often during the day and appeared at the dinner table in a blue . . . kimono with fur-trimmed bedroom slippers. Even in the morning he wore at his side a golden dagger which was

also changed frequently. In his tie pin he wore a variety of precious stones, and around his fat body a wide girdle, set with many stones . . . not to mention the splendor and number of his rings.[26]

Goering's lifestyle contrasted sharply with that of the German Jews. While the Jewish population was being financially ruined by Nazi Germany, Goering was acquiring masterpieces of art that had been confiscated by the Nazis from private Jewish collections. While the Jews were being denied cultural experiences, Goering attended the opera and read widely. Goering had no financial concerns, for in addition to his Reichstag salary, he also received a stipend from the Nazi Party as well as bribes from the business and industrial community who were willing to give him kickbacks in return for lucrative munitions contracts.

In the late 1930s, Goering created the state-owned Hermann Goering Works, an industrial conglomerate that employed 700,000 employees and from which he made a fortune of several hundred million marks. Goering was well liked by the German people, who often affectionately referred to him as the "Fat One."

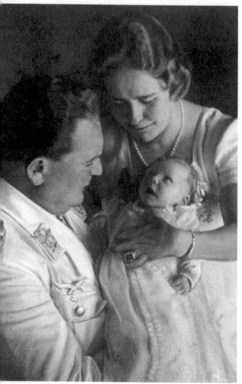

Goering poses with his wife, Emmy, and baby daughter, Edda.

In the spring of 1935, Goering took a second wife, Emmy Sonnemann, an actress from Weimar. Hitler was the witness at their wedding. The Goerings had a mansion in Berlin and used Carin Hall as a country home. Goering established a private zoo at Carin Hall where he kept lion cubs as pets. On June 2, 1938, the Goerings' only child, a daughter, Edda, was born. Hitler was her godfather.

A Well-Kept Secret

Despite his outstanding performance in party and national government and despite his close social relationship with the Fuehrer, Goering knew that to remain in Hitler's favor, he needed to be in complete agreement with Hitler's Final Solution for the Jewish people. This is only one of the many contradictions of Goering's life. Since his schoolboy days, Goering had known that the man for whom he was named, Hermann von Epenstein, was part Jewish. Epenstein's liaison with Goering's mother had produced a son; Goering therefore had a brother who was part Jewish. Goering could have stood up for Epenstein (who by now had died), for his brother, and for all Jewish people. Instead, to further his own personal gain, he complied with Hitler in persecuting the Jews.

Goering fined the Jewish community 1 billion Reich marks for the *Kristallnacht* destruction, of which they had been the victims, and ordered Jewish shopkeepers to repair all broken windows at their own expense. Goering also ordered Jews to wear the yellow Star of David on their clothes. He shut down Jewish businesses and for-

Although named after a Jew himself, Goering (right) stands as Hitler's greatest ally and successor.

bade the Jews from attending public schools or using public recreational facilities. He also prohibited Jews from flying the German flag.

Reich Marshal

Hitler planned the *Anschluss,* a reunification of all the German people throughout Europe. In 1938, Goering orchestrated a German march on Austria. Czechoslovakia, Bohemia, and Moravia were next. Goering was appointed Reich council chairman for national defense on August 30, 1939. The next day, Hitler named Goering his personal successor. When World War II began in 1939, it was Goering's German air force, the Luftwaffe, and its ability to carry out a blitzkrieg ("lightning war") that Hitler credited with the victorious invasion of Poland.

Hitler rewarded Goering with a promotion, which he announced in the middle of a speech to the Reichstag: "As a reward for his mighty contribution to victory, I hereby appoint the creator of the Luftwaffe to the rank of Reich Marshal of the Greater German Reich, and, award him the Iron Cross."[27] Goering began carrying a baton to indicate his promotion.

At first it appeared that Goering and his Luftwaffe could do no wrong. Hitler's confidence in Goering, however, was short-lived. When the British began bombing Berlin, Goering and Hitler disagreed on the method of the London counterattack. In the spring of 1941, when Germany broke its nonaggression pact with Russia, Germany's military machine began to falter. Goering's Luftwaffe failed to successfully invade Russia and to hold off an Allied invasion of the homeland. Hitler blamed Germany's military failures on Goering.

Fall from Hitler's Graces

In 1944, as Hitler and other high-ranking Nazis awaited the Allies' assault on Berlin in a bunker beneath the chancellery building, Goering fled to Bavaria. Upon learning that Hitler had no intention of leaving the bunker, Goering telegraphed Hitler and requested, as Hitler's second-in-command, to be allowed to take over for the Fuehrer. His telegram read:

> Mein *fuehrer,* since you are determined to remain at your post in Fortress Berlin, do you agree that I as your deputy in accordance with your decree of 29.6.41 [June 29, 1941] assume immediate total leadership of the Reich with complete freedom of action at home and abroad? If by 2200 hours no answer is forthcoming, I shall assume that you have been deprived of your freedom of action. I will then consider the terms of your decree to have come into force and act accordingly for the good of the people and the Fatherland. You must realize what I feel for you in these most difficult hours of my life, and I am quite unable to find words to express it. God bless you and grant that you may come here after all as soon as possible. Your most loyal Hermann Goering.[28]

Goering's presumption of his incapacity angered Hitler, who immediately stripped Goering of his right to succession. Hitler accused Goering of betraying the Nazis and demanded that he immediately resign all offices. Hitler ordered his secretary, Martin Bormann, to have Goering executed, but the commandant who was ordered to perform the execution refused to obey Bormann's orders.

Shortly thereafter, on April 30, 1945, Hitler committed suicide. Upon hearing of Hitler's death, Goering said, "Now I'll never be able to convince him that I was loyal to the end."[29]

Cheating the Executioner

Berlin fell to the Allies in May 1945, and that same month Goering was captured. An international military tribunal tried him and other Hitler henchmen in Nuremberg. Goering was charged with conspiracy to prepare aggressive war, crimes against the peace, war crimes, and crimes against humanity. His behavior during the trial alternated between anger and playfulness. He was either directing angry outbursts toward his codefendants or telling jokes.

Goering was allowed to make a statement before the tribunal announced a verdict. He said,

> I never decreed the murder of a single individual at any time, nor decreed any other atrocities, nor tolerated them while I had the power and the knowledge to prevent them. I did not

Goering enters a Nuremberg court to testify before an international military tribunal about his war crimes.

want war, nor did I bring it about. I did everything to prevent it by negotiation. After it had broken out, I did everything to assure victory. . . . The only motive which guided me was my ardent love for my people and my desire for their happiness and freedom.[30]

On September 30, 1946, Goering was found guilty on all four counts and sentenced to death by hanging. His request to die as a soldier by firing squad was denied. On the evening of his planned execution, October 16, 1946, Goering committed suicide by biting down on a poison capsule he had smuggled into his Nuremberg jail cell.

Hermann Goering is a study in contradictions. He carefully cared for the wild animals he kept as pets yet was responsible for millions of human deaths. Cultured and refined in his personal life, he could be ruthless and diabolical in his professional one. Even though he had a brother who was part Jewish, he was part of a regime that was responsible for the mass murder and persecution of millions of people who shared his brother's ancestry.

Hermann Goering will go down in history as Hitler's second-in-command. In only one matter was Hermann Goering fully in command. By taking control of his death, Goering cheated his executioners out of taking his life.

CHAPTER 3

Joseph Goebbels

The German Student Association had been at work in Berlin's public and private libraries all day on May 10, 1933. They cleared the shelves of books authored by those whose names appeared on a list of "subversives" compiled by Dr. Joseph Goebbels, Hitler's newly appointed minister for propaganda and public enlightenment. His list contained the names of almost two hundred Jewish and Marxist authors whose writings opposed the teachings of the Nazi Party.

With hollers and hoots, the students threw the books out library windows and onto the streets, where they were collected and tied in bundles. In Berlin, the bundles were taken to the Franz-Josefsplatz. When darkness fell, piles of books, silhouetted in the moonlight, were set on fire. As the flames illuminated the buildings of Berlin, the students danced around the fire, chanting the names of the authors whose works were being consumed by the inferno.

Members of the Hitler Youth movement participate in a book burning of Jewish and anti-Nazi works.

While the fire was at its brightest, several official cars arrived on the scene. As part of the "celebration of opposition to the un-German spirit,"[31] Goebbels was to address the nation by radio from the Berlin bonfire. Calling the burning of books a "strong, great and symbolic act," he announced the end of the "extreme Jewish intellectualism"[32] that was leading the German people away from pure Aryan ideals.

"The breakthrough of the German revolution has opened the way for what is truly German,"[33] shouted Goebbels. "From these ashes there will arise the phoenix of a new spirit."[34] That night alone, throughout Germany, more than twenty-five thousand books were burned.

Goebbels's techniques of mass persuasion and propaganda brought Hitler to power in the early 1930s. A skilled manipulator and orator, Goebbels is credited with the creation of the "Fuehrer myth," the presentation of Hitler to the German people as a savior. It was the carefully staged theatrics and brazen lies of Goebbels that early on shaped the world's perception of Hitler and the Nazis. As minister for propaganda and public enlightenment, Goebbels was in charge of newspapers, book publishing, and cultural affairs for the Third Reich. Goebbels's deep feelings of inferiority fueled a need for power and control, and in the Nazi Party he found an opportunity to project his self-hatred and rage on a massive scale.

Creator of the "Fuehrer myth," the persuasive Joseph Goebbels served as Hitler's minister for propaganda and public enlightenment.

"Ulex"

Paul Joseph Goebbels was born on October 29, 1897, in the lower Rhine industrial town of Rheydt. His father, Friedrich, worked his way up from errand boy to plant manager in a candle wick factory. Goebbels's mother, Mary Katarina, was a dairy maid. Katarina had almost died giving birth to Joseph, her third son and middle child, and mother and son were extraordinarily close. The Goebbels family was devoutly Catholic, and daily mass and religious devotions were an important part of family life.

Joseph Goebbels was a sickly child, almost dying of pneumonia when very young. At the age of four, he contracted osteomyelitis (inflammation of the bone marrow), which left his left foot deformed. A surgical operation at age ten failed to correct the defect. Goebbels remained small in stature throughout his life. He needed special shoes and braces, and he walked with a limp. As an adult member of the Nazi Party, Goebbels would try to disguise his limp or lie about it, claiming it was a World War I injury.

Goebbels's childhood was lonely and bitter. He felt inferior to other children because his deformed foot prevented him from joining them at play. He became reclusive and hid in his second-floor bedroom, his books his only companions. Of a volume of fairy tales given to him while he was hospitalized, Goebbels said, "These books awakened my joy in reading. From then on I devoured everything in print, including newspapers, even politics, without understanding the slightest thing."[35]

Goebbels compensated for his physical limitations with a desire for learning. At the public gymnasium (the equivalent of an American high school), his classmates called him "Ulex," which means "sly one," because of his uncanny ability to turn every situation to his advantage. Goebbels excelled in all his subjects, but especially favored history. One of his teachers, Christian Voss, lavished extra attention on Goebbels and encouraged him to study German literature and develop himself as a poet. Goebbels would later consider Voss his "first friend in life."[36] Goebbels gave the valedictory address at his gymnasium graduation. After the ceremony, the director of the gymnasium commented that Goebbels would never become an orator. Ironically, it was Goebbels's gift of oratory that is credited with the Nazi seduction of Germany.

When World War I broke out in 1914, Goebbels was almost seventeen years old. He tried to enlist for military service but was turned down because of his foot. The rejection intensified his feelings of inferiority, and the disappointment of not being able to fight for his country remained with him throughout his life. His parents encouraged him to study for the priesthood, but by the time he was ready to go to a university, Goebbels had decided to study German literature and history. In March 1917, Goebbels took the *Arbitur*, the entrance examination for university studies. He did so well on the written examination that he did not have to take the oral exam.

Dr. Goebbels

Although he studied at Heidelberg University on a Catholic scholarship and had joined the Catholic Students Association, Goebbels eventually broke with the Catholic Church. He transferred to several institutes of higher learning before settling at the University of Heidelberg. There he became the student of Professor Friedrich Grindolf, a Jewish literary scholar who was well known for his studies of Goethe. Throughout his university years, Goebbels suffered bouts of depression and in 1920 had a nervous breakdown. In his diary, he categorized this period of his life as "chaos within me."[37]

Goebbels had sufficiently recovered by November 1921, when he received a doctorate in German literature from Heidelberg. Upon receiving his degree, he insisted on being addressed as "Dr. Goebbels." His goal was to be a writer or journalist, and by the time he graduated, Goebbels had written several short books and dramas. One of his novels, *Michael Voorman's Youth*, was autobiographical. Goebbels was unable to get producers for his plays, and the articles he submitted to the local newspaper, the *Berliner Tageblatt*, were rejected. Eventually, Goebbels took a succession of jobs that were both low paying and beneath a man with his academic credentials.

In 1924, Goebbels was invited by a friend, Fritz Prang, to attend activities of the German Nationalist Freedom Party, the organization most Nazi sympathizers had gravitated to when the Nazi Party was banned after the Beer Hall Putsch. Goebbels was at first unimpressed with the group. In June 1924, he wrote in his diary, "You Jews and you Frenchmen and Belgians have nothing to fear from these fellows. I have seldom attended a meeting at which so much drivel was uttered."[38]

In August 1924, while Hitler was still imprisoned in Landsberg Fortress, an attempt was made to unite the German Nationalist Freedom Party with other parties splintered from the Nazis. Goebbels attended a meeting in Weimar, the result of which was the formation of the National Socialist Freedom Movement of Greater Germany. Goebbels became an editor and writer for the organization's newspaper, *Volkische Freiheit* ("People's Freedom"), often quoting Hitler in his articles.

"Adolf Hitler, I Love You"

With Hitler's release from prison on December 20, 1924, the ban on the Nazi Party was lifted, and Hitler went about reestablishing the Nazis. Goebbels was among the first to join the newly reorganized Nazi Party. "Germany's youth has its leader once more. We await his command,"[39] he commented in *Volkische Freiheit*.

Hitler assigned Gregor Strasser, one of the cofounders of the German Workers' Party who was now an SA leader, the job of establishing the Nazi Party in northwest Germany. Working under Strasser in early 1925, Goebbels was appointed the business manager of the Rhineland's

Goebbels stands (back row, sixth from right) with members of the SA.

North District Nazi office. Later that same year, at a meeting of all district leaders from northern Germany, Goebbels met Hitler for the first time. At a second meeting shortly thereafter, Goebbels wrote in his diary, "This man has everything it takes to be a king. The born tribune of the people. The coming dictator."[40]

Goebbels's high opinion of Hitler soon faded as he came under the influence of Gregor Strasser and his brother Otto. The Strasser brothers were involved in a disagreement with Hitler over Nazi Party principles. At one point, Goebbels declared, "the bourgeois Adolf Hitler should be expelled from the National Socialist Party,"[41] but in 1926, realizing that his best opportunity for personal gain lay with Hitler, Goebbels resumed his earlier loyalty, writing in his diary, "Adolf Hitler, I Love You."[42]

Hitler rewarded Goebbels's renewed devotion by appointing him district leader of Berlin. Goebbels was twenty-eight years old and had been a party member less than two years. Although small in stature, Goebbels mesmerized audiences with his powerful voice. His rhetoric, coupled with the theatrical quality of his presentations, made him an influential voice in Berlin. Hitler said of Goebbels, "He possesses the two attributes without which no one could master the conditions in Berlin: influence and the gift of oratory."[43]

Party Propaganda Chief

In 1929, Hitler appointed Goebbels Reich propaganda leader for the Nazi Party. In this position, Goebbels traveled extensively,

bringing Hitler's message of the unification of nationalism and socialism to the people. His talks played on the emotions of the audience and were almost always met with Communists rebelling and
taking to the streets in violent and bloody protests. Goebbels's propaganda presentations were like theatrical productions and were always accompanied by parades, music, and songs prior to the
speeches. Goebbels organized propaganda marches in Berlin, where
storm troopers wore white bandages stained red to simulate blood
around their heads. Press coverage provided the Nazis with public-
ity, bringing in new party members. "He who can conquer the
streets can conquer the masses; and he who conquers the masses
conquers the state"[44] was one of Goebbels's propaganda theories.

Goebbels edited *Der Angriff* ("Attack"), a weekly Nazi Party
newspaper, which he used as a forum to call for the overthrow of
the Weimar government. It was especially directed at "Jewish
Marxists," who were blamed for Germany's defeat in World War I.
The voice of the paper became more radical over the years. Many
times, the publication was suspended for inciting political violence,
which was a punishable offense under the Law for the Protection of
the Republic. Goebbels often appeared in court to answer accusa-
tions of using *Der Angriff* as a means of inciting riots or slanderiz-
ing officials. Although he was found guilty, his lawyer always
managed to have a prison sentence commuted to fines, which
Goebbels claimed he would not pay or arranged to pay in the smallest installments possible.

One of Goebbels's earliest propaganda campaigns involved Horst
Wessel, a twenty-three-year-old storm trooper. A popular Nazi Party
speaker, Wessel commanded a particularly aggressive branch of the
SA. In 1930, Wessel was gunned down by his girlfriend's former lover.
Although Wessel's death was unrelated to party politics, Goebbels
turned Wessel into a martyr for the National Socialist movement and
planned an elaborate memorial for him. However, fearing street violence, authorities banned the funeral. Goebbels retaliated by making
a song Wessel had written the official song of the Nazi Party, and later
the second national anthem. The Horst Wessel *Lied* (song) was sung
at every official Nazi occasion from 1933 to 1945.

Goebbels used every means at his disposal to rally the German people's support for the Nazi Party. In his early day, he used the press and
public rallies to spread Nazi propaganda. As time went on, Goebbels
added radio broadcasts and newsreels and cultural activities to his
propaganda machine. With a group of unemployed actors, he created
the National Socialist Experimental Theatre and sent them on tour
performing a play he had written that had been earlier rejected by the-

aters. Goebbels also organized speeches for Hitler at the Berlin Sports Palace to which hundreds of thousands of tickets were sold.

The July 1932 election gave the National Socialists a majority of 230 votes in the Reichstag, yet President Paul von Hindenburg, knowing Hitler's desire to become a dictator, refused to appoint Hitler chancellor. Goebbels began a campaign of propaganda to swing public sentiment toward Hitler. He published party newspapers twice a day. He had a roster of over one thousand Nazi-trained party speakers whom he could call to campaign on Hitler's behalf. Goebbels prepared an itinerary for Hitler that had him traveling throughout Germany. When Hitler gave speeches, Goebbels arranged for members of the audience to chant "Ein Volk, Ein Reich, Ein Fuehrer" to emphasize that, under Hitler, Germany could be one people and one empire, with one leader. After six months of this concerted propaganda offensive, to which Germans were responding with increasingly greater enthusiasm, Hindenburg's resistance was eventually overcome. On January 30, 1933, Hitler was appointed chancellor of Germany. That evening, Goebbels arranged a memorable torchlight parade to celebrate the event.

Goebbels delivers a speech in support of the Jewish boycott. Though short in stature, Goebbels was renowned for his charisma and oratorical ability.

The Little Mouse General

In 1933, at the age of thirty-five, Goebbels was appointed minister for propaganda and public enlightenment. His responsibilities were expanded to include "all areas involving intellectual influence on the nation."[45] Politics and national elections, festivities for national holidays, state ceremonies, broadcasting, commercial fairs, advertising, and sports were all under Goebbels's control. He ruled the press and broadcast media and oversaw all cultural activities—the cinema, theater, and music. He was in charge of communicating to the German people what Hitler wanted them to know.

Goebbels moved in to an office in the two-hundred-year-old Leopold Palace on Wilhelmplatz and had a staff of several hundred. On his office walls were pictures of the eighteenth-century Prussian leader Frederick the Great, whom he admired. Goebbels approached his new position with utmost seriousness, but behind his back Hitler's other ministers referred to their diminutive colleague as the "Little Mouse General."

Goebbels espoused Hitler's views of propaganda as written in *Mein Kampf:* "The art of propaganda lies in understanding the emotional ideas of the great masses and finding, through a psychologically correct form, the way to the attention and thence to the heart of the broad masses."[46] Goebbels's objective was the "mental mobilization" of the masses. His propaganda was intended to work on the German people until they no longer resisted the Nazi government. The ultimate goal was to acquire for Hitler the unconditional loyalty of the people. Goebbels sought to build the confidence of the Germans so they would see Hitler as bringing to Germany a new beginning—both cultural and political. To reach this goal, Goebbels elevated Hitler to a God-like status and promoted national socialism as a replacement for Christianity.

Goebbels called for *Gleichschaltung,* the "Nazification" of all of Germany. To accomplish

This brochure designed by Goebbels defames communism.

SA members put up anti-Semitic flyers designed by Goebbels's department.

this, he created a Reich Chamber of Culture. Its seven branches consisted of literature, journalism, broadcasting, theater, music, film, and fine arts. Goebbels combined all press organizations into the German News Service and enacted laws allowing only those who could trace a pure Aryan ancestry back to 1800 to work as a member of the press. By 1936, the entire Reich Chamber of Culture would be purged of Jews. Jewish newspapers and publishing houses were closed. Goebbels never forgot the humiliation of the rejection of his early writing, and he sought revenge by enacting the "Editor Statute," which put all editors under the control of the state. Goebbels also had loudspeakers erected in public places so that everybody would be able to hear Nazi speeches. He expanded the network of radio stations and directed the manufacture of small, inexpensive radios so that each household would be able to hear Nazi broadcasts. "The radio belongs to us and no one else. . . . We will place the radio at the service of our ideas, and no other idea shall be expressed through it,"[47] Goebbels lectured.

The Big Lie

Goebbels's anti-Semitism was a product of his involvement in national socialism. At the University of Heidelberg he had studied the works of great German-Jewish authors and poets under a distinguished Jewish professor, but the more entrenched he became in the Nazi Party, the more he embraced Hitler's anti-Semitic views. Goebbels longed to be Hitler's favorite follower, so he needed to make Hitler's beliefs his own. His ambition was singly focused, and the higher Goebbels rose in the Nazi Party, the stronger his anti-Semitic feelings became.

Despite threats of an international boycott of the 1936 Summer Olympics due to Germany's political situation, the International Olympic Committee proceeded with plans to hold the Games in Berlin. Although the government buildings were draped with swastika flags, the Nazi Party had decided beforehand to remain as inconspicuous as possible. They wished to project a peaceful image of Germany to the world. Goebbels's propaganda machine swung into high gear to hide evidence of Jewish persecution. Anti-Semitic signs and publications were removed from the streets. Goebbels arranged for the Reich Broadcasting Company to broadcast the Olympic Games by radio, and he had a documentary movie made of the Games, which was used for propaganda purposes.

Hitler leads (front and left) the Nazi procession into a stadium at the 1936 Olympic games.

Once the Olympic Games had concluded, anti-Semitism was again rampant throughout the country. With each passing year, Jewish citizens were subjected to more restrictions and acts of prejudice. On November 9, 1938, Goebbels gave a rousing speech that culminated in the "spontaneous actions" of *Kristallnacht*. He then censored what the press could report about it.

Goebbels strived for the inhumane goal that is today known as ethnic cleansing. His goal was to make Berlin *Judenrein*, "Jew free." October 1941 marked the first deportations of Berlin's Jews to ghettos and concentration camps. Although several thousand Jews were in hiding in Berlin, Goebbels announced that his goal had been met and claimed it as his greatest political accomplishment.

Goebbels lied to the general public about Jewish persecution and concentration camps, allowing the majority of Germans to look the other way as their Jewish neighbors disappeared and smoke was emitted from factories that produced nothing. When horrifying rumors of the camps' atrocities reached the German civilians, most found the news beyond belief.

A Husband and a Father

In November 1930, Goebbels met Magda Quandt, a Nazi Party volunteer. She was divorced and had one son, Harald. Despite Magda's family's objections over her involvement with a Nazi, the couple married in December 1931. In September 1932, their first child was born. Eventually, the couple would have four more daughters and a son. Goebbels cherished his six children.

Goebbels's position as a Nazi leader eventually allowed the couple to acquire two estates near Berlin—Schwanenwerder on an island in the Wannsee Lake and Lanke on the Gobensee Lake. Magda had excellent taste in decorations and an elegant sense of style. Hitler felt comfortable in her homes, and his frequent visits strengthened the relationship between the Fuehrer and her husband.

Magda was worldly and self-assured. She was at ease in social situations and was fluent in many languages, which helped her husband when the two traveled abroad on state visits. She embraced and supported her husband's political ambitions. Hitler thought highly of Magda and allowed her to negotiate with him for an increase in Goebbels's salary.

But the Goebbelses' marriage was not without its troubles. As the minister in charge of cultural affairs, Goebbels was often in the company of beautiful actresses, and on many occasions he was unfaithful to his wife. Magda confided to Hitler that she wished to divorce Goebbels. Hitler, who did not allow divorce among high-ranking

Goebbels marries Magda Quandt in 1931. Magda supported and aided her husband's political career.

Nazi officials, told Magda that if the couple did not stay married, Goebbels would have to resign his posts. With Hitler's help, the couple reconciled. By saving his marriage, Goebbels ensured his further participation in the building of the Thousand Year Reich.

War of Words

When it came to international relations, Goebbels shared Hitler's view that a war of words could be just as significant as a war with weapons. After Germany's invasion of Poland in 1939, and in conjunction with the Fuehrer's Foreign Ministry, a war of words became the focus of Goebbels's propaganda. The Nazis owned wholly, or in part, 350 newspapers outside of Germany, to which they fed their misinformation. Goebbels also controlled twenty-three secret radio stations, which he used to broadcast thirty-four programs in eighteen languages throughout Eastern Europe. In preparation for Germany's takeover of Czechoslovakia, for example, Goebbels provoked a crisis by publicizing fictitious reports of Sudeten Germans' loss of rights. Another Goebbels ploy was to try to undermine civilians' confidence in their own governments. He ordered pamphlets and leaflets depicting British soldiers in humiliating positions and dropped them into England from German planes. When Germany invaded Russia in 1941, Goebbels had 90 million similar pamphlets dropped behind Russian enemy lines.

Goebbels would not allow the press to report German defeats and insisted stories be filled with heroism and victory. As World War II raged on, the German people, many of whom had been dubious about the enterprise to begin with, became more and more disillusioned. To the outside world it appeared that Hitler had the full confidence of his citizens, but in reality it was because anyone who publicly displayed a negative attitude was arrested and sentenced to death.

Goebbels also gave speeches and radio addresses in which he emphasized faith in Hitler. "Let us surpass one another in our love and loyalty to him . . . and to our faith in his historical mission,"[48] Goebbels challenged the German people. To build up morale, Goebbels fabricated rumors of a new weapon that would be unleashed against the Russians. He rallied support for the German troops by organizing a "Winter Aid" collection of warm clothes for the soldiers fighting in Russia. In July 1944, Hitler named Goebbels "Reich plenipotentiary for total war effort"; as a result, he was given additional responsibilities for the protection of civilians.

Goebbels builds Nazi morale at a book-burning rally by only relaying news of German victory to the people.

The End of a Clever Man

As Russian troops advanced on Berlin in the spring of 1945, Goebbels encouraged the German people to hold out as long as they could. To uphold the people's morale, he hired painters to paint the words "Hatred our duty—revenge our virtue"[49] on the streets of Berlin. Despite the destruction of his ministry office by a bomb on March 13, 1945,

Goebbels and his wife poisoned their children to commit suicide after receiving news of Hitler's death.

Goebbels immersed himself in his work. He reorganized a postwar press and broadcasting structure. He finished a book he was writing titled *Das Gesetz des Krieges* ("The Law of War") and worked on his journals, which he agreed could be published ten years after his death. In April, as Russian troops were closing in, Goebbels joined Hitler in the bunker below the chancellery building. Soon, Magda and their children joined him. On April 29, Hitler drafted his political will and testament, naming Goebbels as his successor. Goebbels added his own appendix to Hitler's document, stating that he would not obey Hitler's command but would follow Hitler to death, as would his wife and children. Goebbels and his wife could not imagine a world without Hitler and were ready to take their own lives if Hitler died.

After Hitler's suicide on April 30, 1945, Goebbels became chancellor and president of Germany for one day. Then on May 1, 1945, Goebbels and his wife poisoned their six children shortly before taking their own lives. Magda poisoned herself and Goebbels shot himself. As per their instructions, Magda and Goebbels's bodies were doused with gasoline, set on fire, and left to burn in the chancellery garden, where the remains were found by the Russians.

Much of what is known about Goebbels comes from his own words—the thousands of pages of diaries he began in his preuniversity days. Goebbels considered his diaries the only authentic and realistic account of the rise of Hitler and Nazi Germany. They constitute twenty-three volumes in total and were discovered by the Russian army after the war. Goebbels's diaries portray him as a man who lacked the capability to show sympathy toward others yet had a desperate need to be admired and loved. In addition, Goebbels could love only those who seemed to love him. Hitler exploited Goebbels's weaknesses and used them to feed his own need for power. Without Goebbels's propaganda, the Hitler myth would never have been successful. Goebbels fully believed in the myth he had created, and because he could not imagine life in a Germany without the Fuehrer, his very creation became the means of his destruction.

CHAPTER 4

Heinrich Himmler

As head of the Gestapo, Heinrich Himmler often made the rounds of the concentration camps. At one camp he noted a young man, about twenty years old, standing in the line leading to the gas chambers. The man had blue eyes and blond hair and looked more Aryan than Jewish. Himmler went up to him and asked him if he was a Jew. The young man said that he was. "Were both your parents Jewish?" Himmler asked. Again, the young man answered, "Yes." "Do you have ancestors who were not Jews?" Himmler asked again. "No," replied the youth. "Then I can't help you,"[50] said Himmler, and the man was led off to be executed.

Chief of the SS and the Gestapo, Heinrich Himmler poses in Nazi uniform.

Heinrich Himmler believed in racial purity. Like Hitler, Himmler believed that purging Germany of "undesirables" would result in a strong Aryan population. Himmler's plan to design a master race led to the deaths of millions. At the peak of his power as head of the Gestapo, the secret police that oversaw the concentration camps, Himmler applied the principles used to strengthen breeds of livestock by "weeding out" the genes of unwanted people. His radical ideas on breeding led to the formation of *Lebensborn,* the state-sanctioned illegitimacy in which young German girls with perfect Nordic characteristics were encouraged to bear the children of SS men, with the offspring of these unions being cared for by the state.

"Heini Will See to It"

Heinrich Himmler, born near Munich on October 7, 1900, was the middle of three sons born to Gebhard Himmler and his wife, Anna, the daughter of a tradesman. Prince Heinrich of Bavaria, after whom Himmler was named, was Heinrich's godfather. From the time he was a toddler, Himmler was a sickly child who suffered from stomach and respiratory infections. When he was six years old, illness forced him to miss so much school that he needed a tutor to catch up. Except for his recurrent illnesses, his childhood was unremarkable.

An unwavering German patriot, Himmler served in several important Nazi posts.

Gebhard Himmler was an educated man who taught in a Munich gymnasium (school) and tutored Bavarian royalty. He spent his evenings reading German classics to his sons. In 1910, young Heinrich Himmler entered the Royal Munich Gymnasium. When his father received the position of deputy head at the gymnasium in Landshut, Himmler and his older brother transferred to their father's school. Academic excellence was stressed in the Himmler family, and the elder Himmler instructed his sons even during the school's summer break. Himmler excelled in his studies, especially history, but did not fare well in gym, because he was plump, weak, and clumsy.

When he was not studying, Himmler played piano, collected stamps and coins, and played chess with his brothers. The Himmler family was close. They spent summers in the Bavarian Alps or Austria, where Himmler swam and hiked. The family was devoutly Roman Catholic and attended mass and other prayer services daily, even while on vacation. Himmler learned from his parents that it was wise to respect important people and to win their favor by obedience.

World War I erupted when Himmler was fourteen years old. He clipped newspaper articles about the war and recorded battles in his diary, listing war details alongside the accounts of his day-to-day life. Himmler was exceptionally patriotic and never once doubted that Germany would be victorious. "I would like, best of all, to be in the middle of it,"[51] he wrote in his diary on August 28, 1914. At age fifteen,

Himmler joined the *Jugendwehr*, an army-preparation organization, and in January 1918 he became an officer trainee in the 11th Bavarian Infantry Regiment at Regensburg. World War I was drawing to a close, however, and Himmler did not receive a commission.

Himmler decided on a career in agriculture and was a new apprentice at a farm in Ingolstadt when he was felled by a bacterial infection that produces symptoms similar to typhus. After being hospitalized he attended a technical high school in Munich, graduating in 1922 with a degree in agriculture. His first position was in Schleissheim as a salesman with a fertilizer company.

A master of tiny details, Himmler took it upon himself to arrange the affairs of others. Order and organization ruled his life. Even from the training camp at Regensburg, he was involved in the goings-on at home. His parents requested his help as they dealt with the day-to-day deprivation the war was inflicting on civilians. When his brother Gebhard was having a problem with his fiancée, Himmler approached the woman on his brother's behalf and ended the relationship. "Heini will see to it" became a family slogan.

A Revolutionary in the Making

The mild-mannered young Himmler who had carried shopping bags for elderly neighbors grew into a rigid and arrogant adult, constantly at odds with family and friends. In conversations, letters, and diary entries, his words became sarcastic and haughty. He tried to project his own harsh standards on others and criticized his mother and older brother for lack of self-control. He pressed his opinions on others in conversation and preached to them when their behavior was not to his liking. When his attitude alienated others, he had periods of remorse and self-recrimination. "I just can't keep my mouth shut," and "when will I stop talking so much?"[52] he wrote in his diary. By 1924, he would be aggressively persuading others to yield to his views.

While in the army, Himmler had attended meetings of the *Bayerrische Volkspartei* (BVP), a Bavarian counterrevolutionary movement intended to stir the peasants against the Communists. Diary entries show that Himmler was depressed about Germany's political climate. The newly formed Weimar Republic was making no improvements in the postwar morale of the German people, and one November 1919 entry reads, "I was awfully serious and depressed. I believe very bad times are coming, or does it mean something else?" A few days later he wrote, "Perhaps in a few years I'll be involved in war and struggle. I'd be so happy with a war of liberation and would go along."[53]

Himmler holds the Nazi flag with the SA during Hitler's Beer Hall Putsch.

Himmler kept lists of the books he read, including a commentary on each one. By the time he was in his early twenties, he was reading books and pamphlets with anti-Semitic themes and was verbally insulting elderly Jews on the streets of Munich. In 1923, Himmler joined a paramilitary unit later called *Reichskriegsflagge* (Reich War Flag) run by Ernst Roehm, a Bavarian army district staff officer who, with Hitler, had been one of the organizers of the Nazi Party. *Freikorps* (volunteer units) such as Roehm's were preparing to overthrow the Soviet republic that had been set up in Munich after the war.

Leaving his position as a salesman in 1923, Himmler joined the Nazis. How and when Himmler met Hitler is not known, but it is likely that Himmler's talent for organization and administrative detail brought him to Hitler's attention. Himmler was critical of middle-class values yet embraced those that were befitting loyal Nazis. He was a hard worker, methodical in his work practices, and did not drink.

A Time of Reflection

Himmler, who had carried a Nazi banner through the streets of Munich in November 1923, was arrested with many others on the night of the Beer Hall Putsch. Because he had served only as a flag bearer, he was not detained in prison. Unemployed, Himmler moved back home in Munich. He spent his time reading and studying French. He also began questioning his faith and by 1924 had broken with the church altogether.

In June 1924, Himmler went to work in Landshut as an office assistant and secretary to Gregor Strasser, who would later become Goebbels's mentor. Hitler's release from prison that year was the catalyst for the reformation of the Nazi Party. Himmler served first as an unpaid speaker for the party and then as the deputy district leader of Lower Bavaria, a central area that was a hotbed of renewed Nazi activity. Two favorite themes of his talks were "National or International Socialism?" and "The Destruction of the German Peasantry." Himmler's work with the Nazi Party strained his relationship with his family, who viewed him as a failure because of his association with the Nazis and his break with the Catholic Church. "This service to the people is bitterly hard and full of heartaches,"[54] he wrote in his diary.

In 1926, Himmler became deputy propaganda leader, a position that allowed him to interact with other men who would play significant roles in the Nazi Party. When Goebbels first met Himmler earlier the same year, he wrote in his diary, "a good fellow and very intelligent; I like him."[55] The deputy propaganda leader position was followed by a promotion to deputy Reichsfuehrer in 1927. Himmler won a seat in the 1930 elections in which the Nazi Party received 107 votes, making it the second largest party in the Reichstag.

A Private Man

In 1926, Himmler met Margarete Boden, a divorced nurse eight years his senior. She ran an alternative medicine clinic in Berlin that focused on healing through homeopathy, hypnosis, and herbs. They married in 1928. At the time, Himmler was working at Nazi Party headquarters in Munich for a salary that would barely support one. Margarete sold the clinic, and the couple purchased a poultry farm outside Munich. Margarete worked the farm while Himmler put in long hours of work and travel for the Nazi Party. The couple had a biological daughter, Gundrun, in 1929 and adopted a son in 1933. Himmler also had two children by a mistress.

Himmler kept his private life separate from his public life. The salary he eventually earned as a high-ranking Nazi allowed Himmler to purchase a villa in Berlin-Dahlem and a small estate in Bavaria, where Margarete and the children lived. He also owned a castle, Wewelsburg, in Westphalia, which he also used as a conference center for high-ranking top-secret SS meetings. As an adult, Himmler continued to be plagued with headaches and stomachaches, and he often turned to astrologers and fortunetellers on matters of health and work.

Reichsfuehrer-SS

Himmler, who had joined both the SA and SS in 1925, was appointed Reichsfuehrer-SS in 1929. In addition to elite guard protection, the SS, which at the time had fewer than three hundred men, was responsible for gathering intelligence both within and outside the Nazi Party. Under Himmler, the SS became independent of the SA. By 1933, when Hitler took over as chancellor, the SS stood at fifty-two thousand members. Himmler wanted the SS to serve as a source of pure Nordic genes from which all of Germany would be revitalized. Thus in 1930, he warned his officers that "the greatest caution must be exercised in enrollment for we want only the best human material."[56] Soon after, Himmler announced an Engagement and Marriage Decree that required SS officers and their wives to prove Aryan ancestry back to 1750.

Himmler's allegiance to Hitler was absolute. "Believe me," he addressed his SS troops, "if Hitler were to say I should shoot my mother, I would do it and be proud of his confidence."[57] Not surprisingly, Himmler insisted on the same loyalty from the SS members, all of whom had to swear an oath to Hitler: "I swear before God this holy oath, that I shall give absolute confidence to the Fuehrer of the German

As Reichsfuehrer-SS, Himmler walks amongst his SS troops during an inspection.

61

Reich and people, Adolf Hitler, the Supreme commander of the Wehrmacht, and as a courageous soldier will be ready at all times to lay down my life for this man."[58]

In the mid-1930s, the number of SS members rivaled that of the Germany army. As if to prove their allegiance to Hitler, the SS played a large part in the raid and subsequent execution of SA members in June 1934 during the "Blood Purge" conducted on the Night of the Long Knives.

Added Responsibilities

In 1934, Himmler became chief deputy of the Gestapo, the secret police that Goering had organized in 1933. Under Himmler, the Gestapo, originally intended as an intelligence-gathering unit for purposes of domestic intimidation, became synonymous with terror. Gestapo *Einsatzgruppen* (task forces) went to the homes of "undesirables" and either killed them on the spot or sent them to concentration camps.

Anyone believed to be harboring anti-Nazi sentiments could be a target, including suspected party dissidents, but Jews and Commu-

As chief deputy of the Gestapo, Himmler (center) tours a concentration camp with SS officials.

nists were the Gestapo's usual victims. The Gestapo had complete authority in any situation it chose to enter. Its power was not restricted by the legal system, and no court of law could challenge its actions. In 1936, Hitler appointed Himmler chief of the German police, which not only put his loyal henchman in control of all the country's uniformed police but incorporated the SS into the Gestapo. Two years later, the SS was given responsibility for the administration of the concentration camps and for overseeing the mass killings conducted at these facilities. "Triangle of Terror" was the name given to Himmler's three spheres of influence: the camps, the Gestapo, and the SS.

Himmler was viewed as a father figure by his SS, a role he relished. The huge number of people the SS were ordered to kill caused many of them to turn to alcohol to dull their senses. Himmler would give them "pep talks." "Most of you SS men will know what it means when a hundred corpses of executed persons lie there, when five hundred lie there, or when a thousand lie there. To have remained unrelenting . . . that has steeled us," Himmler told them in 1943. He went on to acknowledge, however, that they would never be publicly acclaimed as heroes for their gory deeds. "This is a glorious page in the book of our history which has never been written and is never to be written,"[59] he said.

"Work Liberates"

As Hitler's regime settled into power, Germany's prisons could not hold the numbers of anti-Nazi dissidents who were arrested. Communists, Social Democrats, trade union leaders, and members of the Catholic Church were denounced for as little as a comment or a gesture. Primitive concentration camps called "wild camps" were erected by Nazi storm troopers to hold political prisoners for "reeducation" to the Nazi doctrine. "Reeducation" often involved beatings and torture.

In 1933, Himmler oversaw the construction of a new camp at an unused munitions factory in the town of Dachau, twelve miles northwest of Munich. Political prisoners were sent to Dachau without benefit of a trial and often without being told why they had been arrested. They never learned how long their sentences were to be; they were simply incorporated into the camp's system of slave labor. When not working, Dachau prisoners were crammed together in dismal huts. Food was rationed and sanitary facilities inadequate. Many died of disease and starvation. Others were shot or hanged for failure to obey an SS guard command.

Upon entering Dachau, prisoners passed under an iron gate bearing the words *"Arbeit Macht Frei,"* which translates to "work liberates" or "work sets you free." Inmates constructing camp buildings worked

Inmates at the Dachau concentration camp gather to hear Hitler. Dachau became the Nazi ideal of a work-based camp.

as slaves for the SS twelve hours a day. To Himmler, Dachau demonstrated how "undesirables" could be used to serve the master race. After World War II, the Allies found that some concentration camps contained miniature corporations that had been built by slave labor. "Whether nations live in prosperity or starve to death interests me only insofar as we need them for slaves . . . otherwise it is of no interest to me,"[60] Himmler said. Dachau's slave labor system became the model for the Buchenwald, Sachsenhausen, and Ravensbruck concentration camps.

The Fruits of Wannsee

Although death from starvation, disease, and lack of medical treatment was common in the concentration camps from the beginning, the camps were not originally designed for mass killings. It was not until January 1942, at a secret meeting of high-ranking Nazis in the Berlin suburb of Wannsee, that the agenda was set for the "Final Solution" to the "Jewish Problem." By this time, Germany was at war and had occupied many European countries. The Jews of each conquered country became targets. Himmler, to whom the Jews were "the primary matter of everything negative,"[61] was put in charge of the killing of Europe's 11 million Jews, who were to be "rounded up and sent to 'transit ghettos' in the east. . . . Everyone [at the Wansee Conference] endorsed the general policy of exterminating the Jews of

Europe, although no complete consensus had been reached about one single method of accomplishing this goal—shootings, gassings or death through slave labor."[62]

After watching *Einsatzgruppen* massacre a hundred Russian Jews by shooting, Himmler ordered a "more humane"[63] method of killing. The idea of using poison gas had surfaced in 1939, and experiments with Zyklon B, a crystalline form of prussic acid, showed that the crystals could be easily converted to a gas known to be poisonous enough to quickly kill large numbers of people at a time. Gas chambers, cement buildings equipped to administer the poison gas, had been operational on a limited basis since 1941. The directives of the 1942 Wannsee Conference put into practice the use of Zyklon B for mass killing.

Concentration Camps Throughout Europe

Himmler also approved the use of concentration camp inmates as guinea pigs in medical experiments so cruel that no institution dedicated to healing would have ever performed them. As World War II dragged on and Germany was attacked by the British by air, Himmler ordered prisoners to be worked to death building roads and clearing bombed-out cities.

The Final Solution was never referred to as what it really was—the genocide of millions of people. Rather, Himmler used a system of euphemisms in his communications. In a memo to Heinrich Muller, head of the Reich Security Main Office, he wrote of the "large emigration movement" of Jews, adding, "we both know that there is an increased mortality rate with those Jews put to work."[64]

"Faithful Heinrich"

The Blood Purge following the Night of the Long Knives had been Himmler's ticket to a steady stream of promotions in the Nazi Party.

Himmler (right) remained faithful to Hitler and the Third Reich until his death.

He enjoyed Hitler's trust, and in the waning days of World War II, when it was clear that Germany's defeat was only a matter of time, Himmler was put in charge of the political management of occupied Poland. As Jews and other "non-Aryan" people were relocated outside of Germany, Himmler sought to return people of German ancestry back to their native country.

In 1944, Himmler, who lacked any military experience, was made commander in chief of the reserve army. As the Russians were closing in on Berlin in the spring of 1945, Himmler took it upon himself to negotiate with the head of the Swedish Red Cross, Count Folke Bernadotte, for his release and the release of two hundred other Nazis. He offered cash and the freedom of thirty-five hundred Jews held in concentration camps. Himmler saw himself as Hitler's successor and, as such, asked the Swedish government to submit his offer of surrender to the Western Allies. To Himmler's surprise, the Allies would not negotiate with him. When Hitler heard of Himmler's negotiation attempts, he flew into a rage and yelled that "faithful Heinrich" had betrayed him. "A traitor must not succeed me as *Fuehrer*. See to it that he does not,"[65] said Hitler and expelled Himmler from the Nazi Party.

A banished Himmler disguised himself in civilian clothes and, with a black eye patch over one eye, tried to cross the British-American lines to get back to Bavaria. Stopped by guards at a checkpoint, he and two members of his staff were taken to a British prisoner-of-war camp at Seelos-bei Bremervorde, where Himmler gave his name as Heinrich Hitzinger. Eventually, the three were transported to an interrogation camp at Barnstedt near Luneberg, where Himmler admitted his true identity. Captain Tom Silvester, the officer in charge, reported that Himmler "behaved perfectly correctly and gave me the impression that he realized things had caught up with him. He was quite prepared to talk, and indeed at times appeared almost jovial . . . . I found it impossible to believe that he could be the arrogant man portrayed by the press before and during the war."[66] While being searched, Himmler bit down on a cyanide capsule he had been carrying since the beginning of the war and ended his life. Himmler was secretly buried by British soldiers, and the whereabouts of his remains are not generally known.

One of the lessons Heinrich Himmler learned from his parents was to obey his superiors. This allowed him to draw an all-consuming identity from his role in the Nazi Party. Himmler's weak ego provided him with an excuse for the atrocities he committed: He was doing what the Fuehrer asked of him.

CHAPTER 5

Rudolf Hess

At 10:08 on the evening of May 10, 1941, a member of the Royal Air Force Women's Auxiliary Corps at Inverness picked up an unknown airplane on her radar screen. Up and down the east coast of Scotland, volunteers raised their binoculars to see for themselves the twin-engine Messerschmitt ME 110 flying due west at 450 miles an hour. Immediately above its target of Dungavel, the estate of the duke of Hamilton, the plane soared to a height of two thousand meters and then the engine cut off. The plane went into a half-loop, then soared up again, reached a peak, and began to plunge to Earth. By the light of the moon, a single white parachute could be seen drifting slowly from the sky. Rudolf Hess, Hitler's deputy, had landed in Scotland on a self-appointed mission of peace. Hess's loyalty to Hitler and love of Germany were the reasons he embarked on his mission. Hess was a follower, not a leader, but his years as a top Nazi had emboldened him to commit acts few would have thought him daring enough to orchestrate when he first joined the Nazi Party in 1920.

The first time Rudolf Hess heard Adolf Hitler speak at a German Workers' Party meeting, he was awestruck by the wildly gesticulating politician. Hitler was Hess's idea of the perfect dictator, the fuehrer needed to restore Germany and propel it into the future. Hess immediately began to worship Hitler, an adulation that would be the focus of Hess's life for the next sixty-seven years. Hess would give his life for Hitler, but he was not executed. Because he worshiped Hitler, Hess would live in solitary confinement until he was ninety-three years old.

The "Egyptian"

Rudolf Hess was born on April 26, 1894, in Alexandria, Egypt. He was the first son of Fritz Hess, a German businessman, and his wife, Klara. Rudolf's mother, the daughter of a Swiss merchant, was educated and a musician. His paternal grandfather, Christian, had founded Hess and Company, a successful import firm, soon after arriving in Alexandria in 1865. When his father died in 1888, Fritz took over the family business. Immediately after Rudolf was born, his father announced him heir to Hess and Company. Hess had a younger brother and sister. The Hess siblings were raised in a strict, authoritarian German Protestant home ruled by their father.

Of his father, Hess said he instilled "sheer terror"[67] in his children, and Hess admitted to feelings of animosity toward his father, whom he referred to as the "household dictator."[68] Nevertheless, Hess admired his father's authority. His mother, Klara, softhearted and kind, provided balance in the Hess household. She encouraged an interest in music and astronomy in her children. She was a "good complement to father's strong virility in the prime of his life,"[69] Hess wrote many years later.

Hess led a sheltered childhood, and with the exception of summers with his family in the Fichtel Mountains of Germany, he rarely left the family villa in the Alexandrian suburb of Ibrahimieh. Hess was educated at home by tutors until he was fourteen years old; he was then sent to a Protestant boarding school, Deutsches Haus, in Germany. His classmates considered him a foreigner and called him the "Egyptian."

Nazi leader Rudolf Hess (seated) and his siblings grew up in a strict Protestant environment.

"The Soldiers Are Giving the Orders"

Hess showed an ability in mathematics and the sciences, especially astronomy, but his father would hear of no other career for young Hess except the family business. At the age of seventeen, Hess transferred to the Swiss boarding school Ecole Superieure de Commerce. "I wasn't meant for the business world. . . . Business didn't interest me in the least,"[70] he said. Barely passing his classes, Hess took a commercial apprenticeship in Hamburg. Shortly thereafter, Germany declared war on Russia and France. Hess was twenty years old. He refused to continue his apprenticeship and, over his father's objections, volunteered for the Seventh Bavarian Field Artillery

Regiment. "Now the soldiers are giving the orders, not the business-men,"[71] he told his parents.

In September 1914, Hess was transferred from field artillery to infantry and became part of the First Infantry Regiment, one of the most distinguished Bavarian regiments. He was promoted to lance corporal and received the Iron Cross, Second Class, for defense against enemy attack. In 1916, Hess's unit was transferred to the western front to strengthen troops already in position. There he participated in the Battle of Verdun, perhaps the bloodiest battle of World War I. While recuperating from injuries received near Fort Douaumont, Hess twice submitted his application for pilot training to the Imperial Air Corps. Both times he was rejected.

In December 1916, Hess was promoted to vice sergeant and was ordered to Romania as platoon leader. Twice more, Hess was wounded, the second time by a bullet in his lung. While in the hospital, Hess received his commission as lieutenant. In 1918, after recuperating from his injuries, Hess was asked to escort an infantry unit to the western front. While reporting for duty, he came in contact with corporal Adolf Hitler, who was carrying a message to the regiment commanding officer. Although the two took note of each other, they did not speak to one another.

Although Hess had been accepted for flight school upon applying a third time, the war ended before he could serve as a fighter pilot, and on December 13, 1918, he was discharged from the air force. Hess and Company had been seized by the British, and Hess's father's fortune had been reversed. Hess enrolled at the University of Munich to study political economics and the relatively new field of geopolitics, the study of politics from a geographical point of view. One of his professors was Karl Haushofer, a proponent of *Lebensraum*, the theory that called for the annexation of other countries to Germany to increase German "living space." Haushofer was in favor of the creation of a strong German state by the colonization of overseas territories and the annexation of the Ukraine to Germany. He opposed the Treaty of Versailles, which took away territory from Germany. Hitler's later concept of *Lebensraum*, the motive for annexing Austria and invading Czechoslovakia and Poland, came from Hess, who had learned it from Haushofer.

The "Tribune"

After the war, Hess joined the Thule Society, a group that was anti-Marxist, antiliberal, antidemocratic, and anti-Semitic. The group promoted racist German nationalism and offered it to the German people as an alternative to communism. Previously, Hess had shown

Hess (center) idolized Hitler and became an important mentor to the "Tribune."

no anti-Semitic tendencies; now he believed that the Jews were the cause of Germany's World War I defeat. The November criminals he felt were responsible were Jewish Marxists, and as a member of the Thule Society, Hess was ready to fight them. He helped the society gather weapons. He also signed up volunteers for the militia and Free Corps, an organization of ex-soldiers mobilizing to put down Communist uprisings throughout Germany. In May 1919, Hess was shot in the leg as he participated in one such event.

Like many people living in Germany after World War I, Hess felt the need for a strong leader who could strengthen and unify the government. In an essay written while at the university, Hess described such a leader: "Only a man of the people can establish authority. . . . He himself has nothing in common with the mass; like every great man he is all personality. . . . When necessity commands, he does not shrink before bloodshed. . . . In order to reach his goal, he is prepared to trample on his closest friends." [72]

Hess first heard Hitler speak at the Sterneckerbrau beer hall. Mesmerized, Hess listened to the frenzied speaker who was the advertising chairman of the German Workers' Party and who seemed to be the embodiment of the dictator he had described in his essay. Hess was introduced to Hitler by a mutual friend, the editor and publisher of an anti-Semitic magazine. Hess said of Hitler, "He has a rare, upright and flawless character. He is kind-hearted, religious, and is a good Catholic. He has only one goal and that is his country's well-being."[73] From their first meeting, Hess idolized Hitler. Hess referred to Hitler as the "Tribune" and became Hitler's social mentor, helping him refine his manners and wardrobe. He also helped him with his speeches. Hess threw himself wholeheartedly into Hitler's request to put together a National Socialist student group at the University of Munich, where Hess was still a student. He led a student unit of the storm troopers and was put in charge of gathering information about people belonging to opposing parties as well as Nazi Party members.

Hess did not always agree with the Tribune. Years later, his wife Ilse recalled, "Sometimes he would get incredibly angry about something Hitler said or did. But then he would take his bicycle, ride to a secluded part of the . . . garden, and somehow rid his soul of the anger."[74]

Closest Colleague and Confidant

In the Beer Hall Putsch of November 8, 1923, Hess's assignment had been to take hostages. He arrested the minister of the interior and the minister of agriculture and brought them by car to the town

Hitler (left) sits with Hess (center) and other prisoners after the Beer Hall Putsch failure.

of Grosshesselohe. When the putsch failed, Hess escaped to Austria, where he remained in hiding for five months. In April 1924, he turned himself in and was sentenced to eighteen months in Landsberg Prison, where Hitler was already incarcerated. At Landsberg, Hess strengthened his friendship with Hitler, speaking to the "boss" every day. Hitler wrote *Mein Kampf* ("My Struggle") while in prison, dictating it to Hess. Hess put Hitler's thoughts into a logical order, gave Hitler ideas to be included, and edited and typed the manuscript. Many of Professor Haushofer's ideas on *Lebensraum* can be found in *Mein Kampf*.

Upon Hess's early release from prison in December 1924, Haushofer offered him a position as his assistant at the Institute for Geopolitics, with the possibility of promotion to full professorship. Hitler, who had been released a few days earlier, offered Hess a position as his private secretary. Hess accepted Hitler's offer, and the two settled in Hitler's country home near the Austrian border to finish writing *Mein Kampf*. Otto Strasser, the long-time Bavarian socialist, said of Hess, "Hess loved Hitler. Hess was the only true gentleman in Hitler's inner circle. He did everything for Hitler, even things that must have been in sharp contrast with his natural sense of decency and honor."[75] Hitler would introduce Hess as one of his "closest colleagues and confidants."[76]

On December 27, 1927, after a seven-year courtship, Hess married Ilse Prohl. Ilse was growing despondent about her relationship with Hess and was planning to move to Italy to live and work. When Hitler heard of her plans, he "suddenly put [Ilse's] hand in Rudolf's and said, 'haven't you ever thought of marrying this man?'"[77] Hitler and Haushofer were witnesses at the wedding.

Hess kept his work life separate from his private life. When the Hesses entertained, they did not always invite other Nazi Party members. Hess was frugal and was careful with the generous salary he earned as a high-ranking Nazi. He kept his personal expenses separate from his party expenses. He did not drink except when he had to deliver a speech, which he could do only with the fortification of pink champagne. Hess skied, hiked, drove sports cars, and entered airplane flying contests. Summers were spent at the family villa in Reicholdsgrun. In 1937, the Hesses' only child, a son named Wolf Rudiger, was born. The Hesses eventually settled in a large villa in the wealthy town of Harlaching.

A Loyal Deputy

Hitler took control of the Nazi Party after his release from prison. Hess was made director of Political Central Commission, a position that was second only to Hitler and gave him full authority to regulate all

A loyal Nazi Party servant, Hess stands alongside Hitler as he salutes the crowd at a political parade.

party affairs. Then, in 1933, three months after Hitler was made chancellor, Hitler appointed Hess deputy to the Fuehrer. In this position, Hess was able to settle questions of party leadership and make decisions in the name of the Fuehrer. Hess's decisions were always in line with Hitler's goals and Hess did all he could to make Hitler appear infallible. Hess was protective of Hitler and jealously guarded him from all contacts. Alfred Rosenberg, an early member of the Nazi Party and later a Reich minister, said, "You simply can't get through to Hitler because that Hess is always around!"[78] Hess's close relationship with Hitler made him one of the Nazi Party's most powerful men.

In December 1933, Hess was appointed Reich minister without portfolio, a position in which he read and edited the laws and ordinances of all government departments (except foreign and war). Hess signed anti-Semitic laws and decrees that deprived Jews of their basic human rights as well as their rights as German citizens. He signed the March 10, 1935, law that established compulsory military service. Hess was also appointed a member of the Secret Cabinet Council in 1938, and in 1939 Hitler made him second in line to be his successor, after Hermann Goering.

Hess named Professor Haushofer's son, Albrecht, his personal adviser on foreign affairs. When the Nazi Party machine grew too cumbersome to handle alone, Hess hired Martin Bormann, in 1933, to be a "deputy's deputy." As time went on, Bormann began to make party decisions without consulting Hess. By the start of World War II, Hess was being overshadowed by other henchmen, and around the same time, he began experiencing medical problems with his stomach. Yet his doglike loyalty to the Fuehrer never wavered. After President Hindenburg's death when Hitler appointed himself Germany's president in addition to chancellor, Hess commented,

I can say from my knowledge of the person Adolf Hitler that no one can feel more responsible to his conscience and to his people . . . than he. . . . He has proven by his deeds and his life that he is the embodiment of everything good in the German person . . . he is the executor of the will of a higher power![79]

Obtaining *Lebensraum*

As Hitler's deputy, Hess was instrumental in formulating Hitler's plans on expansion based on Professor Haushofer's views on *Lebensraum*. In 1938, Hess signed the so-called *Anschluss* law annexing Austria to Germany. When Hitler began making plans to take over Czechoslovakia, Hess sent Albrecht Haushofer to Prague to negotiate with the Czechoslovakian minister president. Hess himself met with the leader of the Sudetenland German Party. Both Hess and Haushofer negotiated agreements that improved the situation of Germans living in the Sudetenland. However, Hitler, having already decided on a military takeover, rejected the proposed settlements and

A Nazi advertisement announces a speech to be given by Anschluss *advocate, Rudolf Hess.*

ordered the German military to organize a surprise attack on Czechoslovakia. When Haushofer voiced disappointment at Hitler's failure to follow his foreign policy advice, Hess tried to placate the son of his former professor by saying, "The *Fuehrer*'s intricate strategic plans must seem incomprehensible to you at first glance. But, believe me, I know him better than you. He sees far into the future and he will do what is best." [80]

On April 12, 1939, Hess formally accepted the annexation of the Sudetenland to the Third Reich and participated in the administration of the annexed state. After Germany attacked Poland, Hess set up a central Polish government and implemented laws that called for Gdansk and other Polish cities to be incorporated into the Third Reich.

When Britain and France declared war on Germany after the Polish invasion, Hess fell into a deep depression, was close to a nervous breakdown, and continued to be plagued with stomach problems. Hess never wanted to go to war, and he had taken Hitler at his word when he proclaimed in 1936 that, after annexing the Sudetenland, he would make no more territorial claims on Europe. Ilse Hess commented,

> [Hess] foresaw the return to arms as an unhappiness for all European peoples . . . and the entire world. . . . When the die was cast and the war machine was operating, he did everything in its power to bring about a German victory as quickly as possible and with as few losses as possible. He imagined . . . a victory that would . . . begin a long period of peace among nations of equal rights. [81]

The Hess Affair

Hess knew that, despite the ten-year nonaggression pact Hitler had signed with Russia, Germany was planning to invade and conquer it, and then force Britain to accept peace on Germany's terms. Hess believed that Great Britain and Germany should not be fighting against each other but that the two "master Aryan races" should combine forces to fight communism. Hess conceived of a plan to fly to England to negotiate peace with Britain. He had Albrecht Haushofer write to the duke of Hamilton, an officer in the Royal Air Force, inviting him to meet Hess in Portugal to discuss peace. Hess planned to offer the duke an agreement, stating "Hitler is willing to meet with Britain to stop this war with honor." [82] Receiving no response, Hess began making preparations to fly to the duke's estate, Dungavel, near Glasgow, Scotland. When Hitler set the date for "Operation Barbarossa," the Russian invasion, for June 22, 1941, Hess knew that time was running short and an offer to Britain had to be made soon.

Allied soldiers and policemen in Scotland inspect the crash of a Messerschmitt Me 110 plane flown by Hess.

Logging in under the name "Alfred Horn," Hess began practice runs with a Messerschmitt Me 110, a relatively new fighter plane that could travel at speeds of 450 miles per hour. He took along Fuehrer's private pilot on these "relaxation" exercises. Hess's position in the Nazi Party allowed him to obtain a classified-state secret map of restricted air zones. At 6:10 P.M. on Saturday, May 10, 1941, calling his flight an "act of political importance,"[83] Hess departed Haunstatten Airport in Augsburg in a silver-gray Me 110 for the eight hundred-mile trip. Only Hess's adjunct, Karlheinz Pintsch, knew of his mission.

Of the flight, Hess said, "For some moments I thought to turning back. Then I said to myself . . . 'Night landing with this machine is tricky business.'"[84] Hess parachuted onto a meadow near the village of Eaglesham, south of Glasgow, spraining his ankle. He was met on the ground by a farm foreman, armed with a pitchfork, who took Hess to his house.

Identifying himself as Captain Alfred Horn from the German air force, Hess requested to be taken to the duke of Hamilton. Instead, shortly after midnight, Hess was taken to a military base near Glasgow, where he was searched by British army and air force officers, and then moved to an infirmary, where his ankle was set. Hess told his captors he had to speak to the duke of Hamilton, that he had a message that "Hitler was willing to meet with Britain to stop this war with honor."[85] The duke did not visit Hess until the following morning, at which time

Hess could not prove to the duke that he was who he said he was. British intelligence was able to identify Hess, but the duke refused to bring Hess to the king, as Hess was requesting.

A Mission of Humanity

Hess explained that he was "on a mission of humanity and that the *Fuehrer* did not want to defeat England and wished to stop the fighting." [86] Hess's message invited the British to cease hostilities with Germany and join with it to fight Russia. Germany's demands were clear: Hitler would give the British control of their empire, and Germany would control continental Europe and take back its colonies that were surrendered in accordance with the Treaty of Versailles. Britain and Italy must sign a peace treaty, and Churchill had to resign as prime minister, as the Fuehrer refused to negotiate with him. Hess expected the British to greet him and his proposal for peace with open arms. He was offering them an honorable way to stop the war.

Before his departure, Hess left two letters; one was to his wife, the other to Hitler. The letter to Hitler read, "My action must not be interpreted as a sign of German weakness. On the contrary, I shall lay stress on the military invincibility of my country and point out that Germany did not have to ask for peace." [87]

Hitler flew into a rage upon hearing of Hess's flight, and Goebbels immediately fabricated a propaganda campaign aimed at discrediting his colleague and rival. The German radio led off gently with an announcement that Hess, who should not have been flying because of an old illness, had somehow managed to obtain an airplane and taken off from Augsburg, but he had not returned. The German press, however, published the following news item: "Party Comrade Hess lived in a state of hallucination, as a result of which he felt he could bring about an understanding between England and Germany." [88] Later, British newspapers reported that Hess, whom they identified, had parachuted into Scotland and was receiving treatment for an ankle injury in a hospital near Glasgow. Even if the British had been inclined to negotiate with Hess when he first arrived, they would not take him seriously after the Fuehrer of Germany declared him a "deluded, deranged, and muddled idealist." [89] Hess remained incarcerated in the Tower of London until October 6, 1945, when he was transferred to Nuremberg to stand trial with twenty-one other Nazi war criminals.

Hess wrote to his wife from prison: "Of course I didn't achieve anything with my mission. I couldn't put an end to the mad war between nations. I couldn't prevent what happened or what I saw would happen. I couldn't save us, but I am happy that I at least tried." [90]

Hess, the Madman

Some historians believe that Hitler knew about Hess's flight and that the two had an arrangement in which, if Hess's mission failed, Hitler would disavow any knowledge of it and cover up the operation by calling Hess insane. Hess would never say whether Hitler had known. Hess's wife, Ilse, consistently claimed that her husband had acted without Hitler's knowledge. Wilhelm Bohle, a friend of Hess's, however, contradicted Ilse Hess at the Nuremberg trials when he swore under oath that Hess, "who was always over-cautious and shrank from making big decisions, would not attempt an operation of such magnitude without consulting Hitler, much less carry it out."[91]

Hess's biographer, Wulf Schwarzwaller, believes that in a dictatorship such as Nazi Germany, Hitler would have heard beforehand of Hess's preparations to fly to England. It would have been impossible to fly through German air space without an order from a superior officer, and a lower-ranking officer would have risked execution for granting safe passage to Hess. Schwarzwaller concludes, "Hess had arranged his mission so that Hitler never had to officially acknowledge any of the plan, thus leaving him free, in the event of failure, to publicly condemn his deputy and closest friend. Out of blind loyalty, Hess sacrificed himself for the *Fuehrer*."[92]

Trial at Nuremberg

Hess was brought to Nuremberg and tried for his crimes as a high-ranking member of the Nazi Party. During the trial, psychiatrists believed that Hess either was pretending to be insane or was truly

Hess reads in his cell awaiting trial before an international military tribunal.

Hess (front, left) served a forty-year sentence in solitary confinement for conspiracy.

mentally disturbed. When it was time for him to make a closing statement, Hess was rambling and incoherent. He spoke of "the secret forces that made men act and speak according to the orders given them."[93]

Hess stood up for Hitler to the very end, saying at one point, "It was granted me for many years to live and work under the greatest son whom my nation has brought forth in the thousand years of its history."[94] He told the Nuremberg judges that whatever their verdict might be, he expected to one day stand before God and be judged innocent.

Found guilty of conspiracy to prepare aggressive war and crimes against the peace, Hess was sentenced to life in Spandau Prison in West Berlin. The four Allied Powers—the United States, Great Britain, the Soviet Union, and France—took turns guarding Hess and the six other Nazis who were given prison terms. Except for a few months at a British hospital, where he received treatment for an ulcer, Hess remained in solitary confinement. One by one, the other Nazis, even those serving life sentences, were released. Many thought Hess should also be released from prison since he had tried to seek peace. The United States, Britain, and France were willing to release him on humanitarian grounds, but the decision had to be unanimously shared by the four countries, and Russia vetoed each request. One of the Soviet guards explained his country's position: "Our country was devastated, and that devastation was caused by a Nazi hierarchy of which Hess was a vital part. I do not believe that my country will ever agree to the release of Rudolf Hess."[95]

On August 17, 1987, Hess was found dead in his prison cell. At the age of ninety-three, he committed suicide by hanging himself with an electrical cord. He was the longest lived high-ranking member of the Nazi Party.

Rudolf Hess so adored Hitler that he was willing to sacrifice himself to the point of being labeled insane. To his dying day, Hess saw himself as a victim and refused to believe he was a criminal. Although he was not executed as some of the other henchmen were, his life was cut short by the forty years he spent in solitary confinement, and his punishment came to be symbolic of the bondage of German nationhood imposed by blind obedience to Adolf Hitler.

CHAPTER 6

Baldur von Schirach

The stadium at Nuremberg was filled with thousands of young people on a September Sunday morning in 1936. From all parts of Germany they had come, some marching for weeks, proudly carrying their banners and flags. It was Hitler Youth Day, and standing at attention in their uniforms—the girls in white blouses and the boys in brown shirts—the assemblage held the promise of Nazi Germanhood. From the loudspeakers placed strategically around the stadium, an announcement was heard. The Fuehrer had arrived! Amid anthems sung at the top of their voices, drumrolls, and military marches, Adolf Hitler strolled to the speaker's platform, Reich youth leader Baldur von Schirach at his side. "Heil! Heil!" shouted the young people. Schirach walked to the podium and began to address the crowd: "One thing is stronger than you, my *Fuehrer,* that is the love of young Germans for you. . . . We feel ourselves to be chained to your person by your name. Your name is the happiness of the youth, your name, my *Fuehrer,* is our immortality."[96]

Hitler's plan for Germany included an empire that would stretch one thousand years into the future. To ensure the longevity of the Reich, he needed the youth of Germany to embrace national socialism. In 1933, the Fuehrer appointed Baldur von Schirach youth leader of the German Reich. Schirach was twenty-six years old and looked almost as youthful as those over whom he had been put in charge. He organized students and used propaganda to convert them to national socialism. It was the youth that would propel national socialism into the future, and Schirach is credited with bringing hundreds of thousands of youth into the Nazi movement, thereby strengthening the Nazi regime and preparing a country for war.

Yankee Doodle

Baldur von Schirach was born into an aristocratic family on March 9, 1907, in Berlin. He was the oldest of four children. His paternal grandfather had fought as a major in the Union Army during the American Civil War, losing a leg in the Battle of Bull Run. After marrying an American woman, he returned to Germany. Schirach's American grandmother claimed two signers of the Declaration of Independence in her family tree. Schirach's father, Carl Bailey-Norris von Schirach, was a former captain of the Prussian army who later became the administrator of the Court Theatre. Schirach's mother was American. Schirach often whistled "Yankee Doodle" to emphasize the fact that he was three-quarters American.

The Schirach home was filled with culture, and Schirach was exposed at an early age to art, music, and literature. He attended a private school until after World War I, at which time he entered a public grammar school. At age ten, Schirach became a member of the Young Germans' League, a prerequisite to becoming a member of Hitler Youth at age fourteen. Schirach first heard Hitler speak while a grammar school student. He joined the Nazi Party in 1925, as soon as he turned eighteen. Schirach had read *Mein Kampf* and had found that he and Hitler had similar opinions. Schirach called the Fuehrer the "greatest German of all time" and "Germany's greatest son."[97]

As a young man, Baldur von Schirach brought thousands of young people into the arms of the Nazi Party.

Hitler was flattered to have a member of the aristocracy as a follower, and he encouraged Schirach to attend the University of Munich, where he studied German and art history and showed an aptitude for poetry. After Hitler visited the Schirach family in 1925, Schirach's father also joined the Nazi Party. World War I had reversed the elder Schirach's fortunes, making him a willing disciple of the principles of Hitler's national socialism.

Youth Leader

While a university student, Schirach joined the SA. He also denounced Christianity. After joining the National Socialist Student Association,

Schirach (right) stands with "Germany's greatest son" at a Hitler Youth rally.

Schirach became the association's spokesperson for the upper middle class. Hitler endorsed Schirach's promotion to Reichsfuehrer of the association in 1928, and in 1931 he was made Reich youth leader of the Nazi Party, a position that gave him authority over all youth organizations, including Hitler Youth. In 1934, Schirach published a book outlining his agenda for endowing an entire generation with the four Nazi principles: obedience, character, discipline, and leadership. These characteristics were the building blocks upon which the "master Aryan race" would be built.

Schirach organized demonstrations throughout Germany as a means of recruiting young people. When Hitler was appointed chancellor, twenty-six-year-old Schirach was promoted to youth leader of the Third Reich. Schirach succeeded in having Hitler decree a Hitler Youth Law in December 1936 that made his youth organizations, previously under the Ministry of Education, an independent ministry, requiring Schirach to answer only to Hitler or Hess. The law stated that "the whole of German youth within the borders of the Reich is organized in the Hitler Youth. All German Young People, apart from being educated at home and at school, will be educated in the Hitler Youth physically, intellectually, and morally in the spirit of National Socialism to serve the nation and the community," and "the task of educating German Youth in the Hitler Youth is being entrusted to the Reich Leader of the German Youth in the NSDAP [Nazi Party]."[98] Non-Nazi youth organizations were outlawed.

Schirach was determined to obliterate all existing youth organizations, including state- and religious-sponsored groups. Schirach had been personally appointed to "project National Socialism through Germany youth into eternity."[99] Within weeks of his promotion, he staged a raid on the Reich Committee of German Youth Organizations, seizing its records. Youth organizations that refused to merge with Schirach's were dissolved. By 1938, the number of youth enrolled in Nazi-sponsored youth organizations in Germany was over 7 million. Membership was voluntary, until Hitler's second Youth Law decreed in 1939 made participation mandatory. At that time, an additional 4 million youth joined Hitler Youth. Parents were heavily fined if they prohibited their children from participating.

Schirach took seriously his mission of bringing national socialism into the next generation. He told his young followers, "A single will leads the Hitler Youth. The commanding power of every Hitler Youth leader, whether of the smallest or biggest of its units, is absolute—that is he has the unlimited right to issue orders, because he bears unrestricted responsibility. An organization of young people can be successful only if it unreservedly accepts the authority of its leaders. The

Schirach proudly salutes his own Hitler Youth at a Nuremberg parade.

success of National Socialism is based upon discipline."[100] To underscore his dedication, Schirach often had pictures taken with members of the Hitler's Youth and had them posted in prominent places.

"Fuehrer Command, We Follow"

Hitler's interest in developing a youth division of the Nazi Party grew after he became party head in 1921. In February 1922, he announced that the SA would organize a youth section. Its purpose would be to encourage participation in party activities by Germans too young to be admitted in the SA. In March 1922, a proclamation stated that the new Youth League of the National Socialist Party "will educate its members in the same spirit which characterizes the party. . . . Our youth will receive the best possible training for their difficult task in the future. Upon their shoulders rests the future of our Fatherland."[101]

Under Schirach, the Hitler Youth organizations became defined. On March 15 of the year a boy turned ten, he was provisionally eligible to enter *Deutsche Jungvolk* (German Young People). The boy's family was investigated and his lineage certified. Only boys with no trace of Jewish blood could be members. If his ancestry was "pure," he could become a member. Induction usually took place once a year on April 20, Hitler's birthday. A boy was required to swear the following oath: "In the presence of this blood banner, which represents our *Fuehrer*, I swear to devote all my energies and my strength to the savior of our country, Adolf Hitler. I am willing and ready to give up my life for him, so help me God."[102]

When a boy turned fourteen, he could join Hitler *Jungend*, the Hitler Youth proper. This senior branch of Hitler Youth was open only to Aryans between the ages of fourteen and eighteen. Membership requirements were the "love of one's country and people, enjoyment of honest open combat, and of healthy physical activity, the veneration of ethical and spiritual values and the rejection of those values originating from Jewry."[103] Patriotism, physical fitness, violence, and anti-Semitism, typical of Nazi orthodoxy, were the same qualities the Nazis looked for when recruiting.

The activities of Hitler Youth took precedence over schooling. Hitler did not want a society of intellectuals. "A violently active, dominating brutal youth—that is what I am after. I will have no intellectual training. Knowledge is ruin to my young men,"[104] said Hitler. The

Members of the Hitler Youth fervently honor Hitler at a Nazi rally. The youth were trained in military rather than intellectual skills.

Hitler Youth organizations recognized no class, occupation, or social standing. Spirit was to be cultivated by weekly "home" meetings in out-of-the-way places such as basements, where the members would hear lectures and participate in discussions. Hikes and games involving physical fitness were emphasized. The boys wore uniforms of brown shirts and swastika armbands, and each carried his own white flag with an anchor and swastika in the center. Members sang songs with lyrics that proclaimed, "Today we own Germany, tomorrow the whole world." Schirach composed an official youth anthem, and the motto of the Hitler Youth was "Fuehrer command, we follow."[105] Schirach also wrote songs and prayers for the Hitler Youth to sing and recite at their meetings.

Hitler Youth in Action

Bruno Manz, who was a member of Hitler Youth, recalled his experiences in the book *A Mind in Prison: The Memoir of a Son and Soldier of the Third Reich*. He remembers his participation in the organization as happy days of camping in the country. But in addition to time spent singing around the campfire, the German teens were being molded to Hitler's specifications. Above all, Hitler Youth were trained to be fighters. Manz recalls,

> He [the leader] trained us in all sorts of military skills, such as small caliber shooting or throwing hand-grenades. . . . We performed war games such as smuggling a suitcase, which was supposed to contain a bomb, into the railway station. We were always divided into two parties battling each other and [the leader] pushed us to ever more aggressive fighting. Once my group had to storm a steep embankment that was defended by another group. When I had made it almost to the top, one of the defendants hit me with his infantry spade so hard under the nose that I needed medical attention.[106]

A girls' division of the Hitler Youth was created in 1925. Girls ages ten to fourteen joined *Jungmaedel*, the Young Maidens. They wore a uniform of a white blouse, blue skirt, socks, and marching boots. The girls went on long marches on the weekends and were instructed in Nazi philosophy. At age fourteen, girls became members of *Bund Deutscher Maedel* (German Girls League), in which the role of women as producers of healthy German children for the Reich was emphasized. Between the ages of eighteen and twenty-one, the young women worked on a farm, where they helped around the house and in the fields.

The Hitler Youth also indoctrinated young girls into the Nazi party to become producers of Aryan children.

Hitler Youth served Hitler's need for propaganda in indoctrinating Germany's young people into the ways of national socialism. They participated in parades and propaganda marches on Nazi holidays and attended SA rallies. At the 1929 party rally at Nuremberg, two thousand Hitler Youth from across the country paraded past Hitler, arms raised in Nazi salutes. The contingent of youth from Berlin had marched four hundred miles from Berlin in what became known as the Adolf Hitler *Marsch*. High-ranking SA leaders supervised all public appearances of the Hitler Youth.

Hitler Youth at War

With the advent of war, many Hitler Youth leaders were drafted. Older Hitler Youth members who were not yet of draft age took over as leaders, having as many as five hundred charges reporting to them. Becoming victorious in war became the new purpose of Hitler Youth. Members delivered draft notices and ration cards

Schirach began Adolf Hitler schools like this one to develop future Nazi Party leaders for the Third Reich.

and collected scrap metal. They also served as air raid wardens and were trained as firefighters to put out fires caused by bomb- ings. Young Maidens helped in hospitals and schools and served refreshments to troops as they were boarding trains to be sent to the front. As the number of men eligible to fight dwindled, Hitler Youth were called to train and fight in battle. Millions lost their lives in combat during World War II.

Adolf Hitler Schools

Schirach, wanting to establish special leadership schools for the party, created the Adolf Hitler schools. They were free schools whose purpose was to groom future leaders for the Nazis, espe- cially Hitler Youth. On April 20, 1937, Schirach, in a joint effort with Dr. Robert Ley, an alcoholic chemist who held a variety of labor and education positions in the Third Reich, opened an Adolf Hitler school in Crossinsee in Pomerania. Importance was placed on the subject of political science and physical training. Academic courses emphasized practical applications over intellectual stan- dards. Most subjects, taught by Hitler Youth leaders, were geared toward the technical and military. Students were taught how to box and how to handle motorized vehicles, participated in war games, and were given shooting practice.

The Adolf Hitler schools were originally established to attract the brightest twelve-year-olds in the Reich, but the students enrolled eventually came from a cross-section of German backgrounds. The one constant among all pupils was a racially pure background. By 1942, eleven Adolf Hitler schools had been established. Overall, these institutions provided their students with concentrated doses of Nazi ideology, shortchanging them in the knowledge needed for a well-rounded, balanced education. As one former student said, the students were "used up and destroyed as a generation by Adolf Hitler."[107]

The Love of Adolf Hitler

Schirach never wavered in his hero worship of Hitler. "Loyalty is everything and everything is the love of Adolf Hitler,"[108] he wrote. The youth leader fancied himself a poet and used his art to remind the man history regards as a monster of his love and devotion:

That is the greatest thing about him
That he is not only our Leader but a great hero,
But himself, upright, firm and simple,
. . . in him rest the roots of our world.
And his soul touches the stars,
And yet he remains a man like you or me.[109]

The scholarly Schirach used his skill with words to demonstrate his fanatic devotion to Hitler.

Instilling in German youth the foundations of Nazism was in essence worshiping Hitler. Hitler Youth members started their day by pledging allegiance to the Fuehrer. "I promise in the Hitler Youth to do my duty at all times in love and faithfulness to help the Fuehrer so help me God,"[110] they recited. By 1937, Schirach was able to exert control over 90 percent of German youth, and adults and young people alike were revering him as a god, attention he did not discourage.

District Leader of Vienna

When World War II started, Schirach enlisted in the German army as a corporal. He was eventually promoted to lieutenant and received the Iron Cross in France. From 1940 to 1945, Schirach served as district leader of Vienna, the most important Nazi position in Vienna. Schirach and his wife, Henny, the daughter of Heinrich Hoffman, Hitler's personal photographer, and their four children moved to the governor's mansion. During this time he administered the Viennese theaters and opera houses. He was also Reich defense commissioner during this time period, which allowed him to take part in planning the war economy.

As a child from an aristocratic family, Schirach had had only limited interactions with Jews. Around the time he joined the Nazi Party, at the age of eighteen, Schirach began reading anti-Semitic books and literature. One of the books that inspired his anti-Semitism was *The International Jew,* by Henry Ford. (The book was later denounced by its author.) After meeting Hitler, Schirach became a confirmed anti-Semite. In 1942, as the administrator of Vienna, Schirach stated that the relocation of Jews to the east would "contribute to European Culture,"[111] and he oversaw the deportation of sixty thousand Jews to Poland. He also coordinated the slave labor program in Vienna. For these actions, as well as his position as Reich youth leader, at the conclusion of the war, Schirach was tried at Nuremberg with other high-ranking Nazis.

Schirach Denounces Hitler

At the Nuremberg trials, Schirach admitted to misleading the youth of Germany and to ordering the deportations of Jews. He claimed not to know how Germans could commit the atrocities reported by survivors of the concentration camps. He also denounced Hitler. "Before 1934, he was human, from 1934 to 1938 he was superhuman and from 1938 on he was inhuman and a tyrant. . . . About 1942 I began to notice that he was becoming insane,"[112] Schirach said at his trial.

Schirach (right) admitted to poisoning the minds of German youth before the Nuremberg Military Tribunal.

Schirach also said he would bear the guilt of educating young people for a man who "committed murder millionfold."[113] The Nuremberg Tribunal found Schirach guilty of crimes against humanity and sentenced him to twenty years' imprisonment at Spandau Prison. Schirach was released in 1966 and died in 1974.

Baldur von Schirach did not operate concentration camps or gas chambers, nor did he drag people from their beds in the middle of the night and shoot them. But in many ways, he could be considered the most dangerous Nazi of all because of his efforts to indoctrinate German youth. Youth is the promise of every nation, and by word and example Schirach demonstrated and endorsed to the youth of Germany the worst of humankind. Whether he truly realized the error of his ways or denounced Hitler to save his own life, Baldur von Schirach will forever be remembered as the Nazi henchman who dishonored his country by poisoning its youth.

NOTES

Introduction: "Yes, My Fuehrer"

1. Sydney Gruson, "Hitler Dead in Chancellery, Nazis Say . . . ," *New York Times*, May 2, 1945, p. 1.

2. Quoted in Robert Payne, *The Life and Death of Adolf Hitler.* New York: Praeger, 1973, p. 53.

3. Quoted in Louis L. Snyder, *Hitler's Elite: Shocking Profiles of the Reich's Most Notorious Henchmen.* New York: Berkeley Books, 1989, p. 151.

4. William L. Shirer, *The Rise and Fall of the Third Reich: A History of Nazi Germany.* New York: Simon and Schuster, 1960, p. 149.

5. Quoted in Robert Wistrich, *Who's Who in Nazi Germany.* New York: Routledge, 1995, p. 79.

Chapter 1: The Third Reich of a Thousand Years

6. Albert Speer, *Inside the Third Reich: Memories.* New York: Macmillan, 1970, p. 18.

7. Quoted in Wulf Schwarzwaller, *Rudolph Hess: The Last Nazi.* Bethesda, MD: National Press, 1988, p. 97.

8. Quoted in Robert Holland, *Adolf Hitler: A Biography.* New York: Thor Publications, 1966, p. 43.

9. Quoted in Leonard Mosley, *The Reich Marshall: A Biography of Hermann Goering.* Garden City, NY: Doubleday, 1974, p. 9.

10. Quoted in Shirer, *The Rise and Fall of the Third Reich,* p. 70.

11. Klaus P. Fischer, *Nazi Germany: A New History.* New York: Continuum, 1995, p. 26.

12. Quoted in Payne, *The Life and Death of Adolf Hitler,* p. 71.

13. Quoted in Mordecai Paldiel, *Saving the Jews.* Rockville, MD: Schreiber, 2000, p. 16.

14. Quoted in Shirer, *The Rise and Fall of the Third Reich,* p. 484.

15. Quoted in Shirer, *The Rise and Fall of the Third Reich,* p. 485.

16. Quoted in Shirer, *The Rise and Fall of the Third Reich,* p. 599.

Chapter 2: Hermann Goering

17. Quoted in Mosley, *The Reich Marshall,* p. 149.

18. Quoted in Mosley, *The Reich Marshall*, p. 4.

19. Quoted in Mosley, *The Reich Marshall*, p. 9.

20. Quoted in Snyder, *Hitler's Elite*, p. 3.

21. Quoted in Mosley, *The Reich Marshall*, p. 9.

22. Quoted in Mosley, *The Reich Marshall*, p. 41.

23. Quoted in Roger Manvell and Heinrich Fraenkel, *Goering*. New York: Simon and Schuster, 1962, p. 44.

24. Quoted in Mosley, *The Reich Marshall*, p. 144.

25. Quoted in Snyder, *Hitler's Elite*, p. 12.

26. Quoted in Eileen Pearson, *Hitler's Reich*. St. Paul, MN: Greenhaven Press, 1980, p. 24.

27. Quoted in Mosley, *The Reich Marshall*, p. 255.

28. Quoted in Manvell and Fraenkel, *Goering*, p. 135.

29. Quoted in Snyder, *Hitler's Elite*, p. 16.

30. Quoted in Mosley, *The Reich Marshall*, p. 136.

Chapter 3: Joseph Goebbels

31. Quoted in Helmut Heiber, *Goebbels*. New York: Hawthorne Books, 1972, p. 173.

32. Quoted in Roger Manvell and Heinrich Fraenkel, *Dr. Goebbels: His Life and Death*. New York: Simon and Schuster, 1960, p. 125.

33. Quoted in Viktor Reimann, *Goebbels: The Man Who Created Hitler*. Garden City, NY: Doubleday, 1976, p. 181.

34. Quoted in Manvell and Fraenkel, *Dr. Goebbels*, p. 125.

35. Quoted in Ralf Georg Reuth, *Goebbels*. New York: Harcourt Brace, 1990, p. 9.

36. Quoted in Reuth, *Goebbels*, p. 13.

37. Quoted in Reuth, *Goebbels*, p. 30.

38. Quoted in Reuth, *Goebbels*, p. 55.

39. Quoted in Reuth, *Goebbels*, p. 61.

40. Quoted in Reuth, *Goebbels*, p. 67.

41. Quoted in Snyder, *Hitler's Elite*, p. 90.

42. Quoted in Snyder, *Hitler's Elite*, p. 90.

43. Quoted in Manvell and Fraenkel, *Dr. Goebbels*, p. 65.

44. Quoted in Reimann, *Goebbels*, p. 79.

45. Quoted in Reuth, *Goebbels*, p. 55.

46. Adolf Hitler, *Mein Kampf*. Boston: Houghton Mifflin, 1971, p. 180.

47. Quoted in Reuth, *Goebbels*, p. 177.

48. Quoted in Reimann, *Goebbels*, p. 305.

49. Quoted in Reuth, *Goebbels*, p. 346.

Chapter 4: Heinrich Himmler

50. Quoted in Snyder, *Hitler's Elite*, p. 34.

51. Quoted in Bradley F. Smith, *Heinrich Himmler: A Nazi in the Making*. Stanford, CA: Hoover Institution Press, 1971, p. 36.

52. Quoted in Smith, *Heinrich Himmler*, p. 117.

53. Quoted in Smith, *Heinrich Himmler*, p. 89.

54. Quoted in Smith, *Heinrich Himmler*, p. 136.

55. Quoted in Peter Padfield, *Himmler*. New York: Henry Holt, 1990, p. 84.

56. Quoted in Padfield, *Himmler*, p. 110.

57. Quoted in Snyder, *Hitler's Elite*, p. 99.

58. Quoted in Snyder, *Hitler's Elite*, p. 31.

59. Quoted in Wistrich, *Who's Who in Nazi Germany*, p. 114.

60. Quoted in Daniel Jonah Goldhagen, *Hitler's Willing Executioners: Ordinary Germans and the Holocaust*. New York: Alfred A. Knopf, 1996, p. 458.

61. Quoted in Goldhagen, *Hitler's Willing Executioners*, p. 412.

62. Fischer, *Nazi Germany*, p. 506.

63. Quoted in Wistrich, *Who's Who in Nazi Germany*, p. 112.

64. Quoted in Richard Breitman, *Architect of Genocide: Himmler and the Final Solution*. New York: Alfred A. Knopf, 1991, p. 6.

65. Quoted in Snyder, *Hitler's Elite*, p. 37.

66. Quoted in Breitman, *Architect of Genocide*, p. 8.

Chapter 5: Rudolf Hess

67. Quoted in Schwarzwaller, *Rudolph Hess*, p. 43.

68. Quoted in Schwarzwaller, *Rudolph Hess*, p. 44.

69. Quoted in Schwarzwaller, *Rudolph Hess*, p. 45.

70. Quoted in Schwarzwaller, *Rudolph Hess*, p. 53.

71. Quoted in Schwarzwaller, *Rudolph Hess*, p. 55.

72. Quoted in Schwarzwaller, *Rudolph Hess*, p. 48.

73. Quoted in Schwarzwaller, *Rudolph Hess*, p. 94.

74. Quoted in Schwarzwaller, *Rudolph Hess*, p. 97.

75. Quoted in Schwarzwaller, *Rudolph Hess*, p. 116.

76. Quoted in Schwarzwaller, *Rudolph Hess*, p. 117.

77. Quoted in Schwarzwaller, *Rudolph Hess*, p. 118.

78. Quoted in Schwarzwaller, *Rudolph Hess*, p. 184.

79. Quoted in Schwarzwaller, *Rudolph Hess*, p. 150.

80. Quoted in Schwarzwaller, *Rudolph Hess*, p. 173.

81. Quoted in Schwarzwaller, *Rudolph Hess*, p. 184.

82. Quoted in Snyder, *Hitler's Elite*, p. 73.

83. Quoted in Schwarzwaller, *Rudolph Hess*, p. 189.

84. Quoted in Snyder, *Hitler's Elite*, p. 73.

85. Quoted in Snyder, *Hitler's Elite*, p. 73.

86. Quoted in Shirer, *The Rise and Fall of the Third Reich*, p. 835.

87. Quoted in Snyder, *Hitler's Elite*, p. 76.

88. Quoted in Shirer, *The Rise and Fall of the Third Reich*, p. 838.

89. Quoted in Shirer, *The Rise and Fall of the Third Reich*, p. 838.

90. Quoted in Schwarzwaller, *Rudolph Hess*, p. 195.

91. Quoted in Schwarzwaller, *Rudolph Hess*, p. 207.

92. Schwarzwaller, *Rudolph Hess*, p. 219.

93. Quoted in Snyder, *Hitler's Elite*, p. 79.

94. Quoted in Wistrich, *Who's Who in Nazi Germany*, p. 106.

95. Quoted in Snyder, *Hitler's Elite*, p. 82.

Chapter 6: Baldur von Schirach

96. Quoted in Snyder, *Hitler's Elite*, p. 155.

97. Quoted in Snyder, *Hitler's Elite*, p. 151.

98. Quoted in Fischer, *Nazi Germany*, p. 346.

99. Quoted in Snyder, *Hitler's Elite*, p. 154.

100. Quoted in Snyder, *Hitler's Elite*, p. 155.

101. Quoted in H.W. Koch, *The Hitler Youth: Origins and Development 1922–1945*. New York: Stein and Day, 1975, p. 48.

102. Quoted in Shirer, *The Rise and Fall of the Third Reich*, p. 253.

103. Quoted in Koch, *The Hitler Youth*, p. 48.

104. Quoted in Snyder, *Hitler's Elite*, p. 150.

105. Quoted in Fischer, *Nazi Germany*, p. 347.

106. Bruno Manz, *A Mind in Prison: The Memoir of a Son and Soldier of the Third Reich*. Washington, DC: Brassey's, 2000, p. 54.

107. Quoted in Fischer, *Nazi Germany*, p. 354.

108. Quoted in Wistrich, *Who's Who in Nazi Germany*, p. 222.

109. Quoted in Snyder, *Hitler's Elite*, p. 151.

110. Quoted in Koch, *The Hitler Youth*, p. 112.

111. Quoted in Wistrich, *Who's Who in Nazi Germany*, p. 223.

112. Quoted in Snyder, *Hitler's Elite*, p. 161.

113. Quoted in Snyder, *Hitler's Elite*, p. 162.

CHRONOLOGY

1918
November 11: World War I comes to an end.

1919
June: The Treaty of Versailles is signed. Adolf Hitler joins the German Workers' Party.

1921
Hitler takes over the German Workers' Party and changes it to the Nazi Party.

1923
November 8: The Beer Hall Putsch occurs in Munich. Hitler is arrested and sent to Landsberg Prison; while there, he writes *Mein Kampf*.

1924
December 20: Hitler is released from Landsberg Prison.

1929
The U.S. stock market crashes.

1932
July: The Nazi Party becomes the strongest political party in Germany.

1933
January 30: Hitler is appointed chancellor of Germany.
February 27: A fire breaks out in the Reichstag building.
March: The Enabling Act is passed, giving Hitler dictatorial powers.
May 10: Book burnings occur throughout Germany.

1934
June 30: During the Night of the Long Knives, hundreds of SA members are executed by the SS.
August 2: President Paul von Hindenburg dies; Hitler combines the positions of chancellor and president.

1935
September 15: The Nuremberg Laws are enforced.

1936
German troops move into the Rhineland.

1938
March 13: Austria is annexed to Germany (*Anschluss*).

November 9: *Kristallnacht* marks the beginning of an increase in anti-Semitic terror by the Nazis.

1939

April 12: Germany annexes the Sudetenland and invades the rest of Czechoslovakia soon after.

August: Germany signs a ten-year nonaggression pact with the Soviet Union.

September 1: Germany invades Poland.

September 3: Britain and France declare war on Germany.

1940

April 9: Germany invades Denmark and Norway.

May 10: Germany invades Belgium, France, and Holland.

September: Italy, Japan, and Germany form the "Pact of Steel."

The first inmates are incarcerated at Auschwitz.

1941

April 6: Germany invades Yugoslavia and Greece.

May 10: Rudolf Hess flies to Scotland on a mission of peace.

June 22: Germany invades the Soviet Union.

September 19: All Jews older than six are ordered to wear a yellow Star of David.

December 7: Japan attacks the United States at Pearl Harbor.

1942

January 20: The Wannsee Conference meets to discuss the "Final Solution."

November: The Germans take Stalingrad.

1944

June 6 (D day): Americans land at Normandy Beach in France.

1945

January: Nazis force Auschwitz inmates on a death march.

April 30: Hitler commits suicide.

May 7: Germany surrenders to the Allies.

November 20: The Nuremberg trials begin.

1946

Nazi war criminals are executed.

FOR FURTHER READING

David Adler, *We Remember the Holocaust.* New York: Henry Holt, 1989. Holocaust survivors tell their stories in their own words. Contains original photographs from private collections.

Inge Auerbacher, *I Am a Star.* New York: Penguin Putnam, 1986. The true story of a young German Jewish girl who was sent to a concentration camp in Czechoslovakia. An award-winning book of the International Center for Holocaust Studies of the B'nai Brith Anti-Defamation League.

Eleanor H. Ayer, *The Holocaust Memorial Museum: America Keeps the Memory Alive.* New York: Dillon Press, 1995. A section-by-section tour of the Holocaust Museum in Washington, D.C. Includes pictures of the exhibits.

Ann Byers, *The Holocaust: An Overview.* Berkeley Heights, NJ: Enslow, 1998. This book covers all aspects of the Holocaust and the murder of 6 million Jews.

Anne Frank, *The Diary of a Young Girl.* Upper Saddle River, NJ: Prentice Hall, 1993. A classic among Holocaust literature, Anne's diary, written while she was a teenager in hiding in Holland during the Holocaust, has come to be symbolic of all the lives lost. It was discovered after her death, by her father, when he returned to their hiding place.

David K. Fremon, *The Holocaust Heroes.* Berkeley Heights, NJ: Enslow, 1998. As the Nazis were declaring areas "Jew-free," thousands of Jews were being helped by those opposed to the dictatorship regime. These are stories of people who made a difference in the lives of Jews and others on Hitler's "extermination" list.

Eleanor Ramrath Garner, *Eleanor's Story: An American Girl in Hitler's Germany.* Atlanta: Peachtree, 1999. Nine-year-old Eleanor Ramrath's father received an offer of a job in Germany. When war broke out, the family was unable to return to America. This true story describes the family's separation, their starvation, the bombings, and the Allied invasion of Berlin.

Ted Gottfried, *Nazi Germany: The Face of Tyranny.* Brookfield, CT: Twenty-First Century Books, 2000. An exploration of the political and social climate of Germany before, during, and after Hitler's rise to power.

Trish Marx, *Echoes of World War II.* Minneapolis, MN: Lerner, 1994. Stories of the struggles experienced by four children who grew up during World War II. Though their stories are ones of sadness, they are also ones of hope.

Milton Meltzer, *Rescue: The Story of How Gentiles Saved Jews in the Holocaust.* New York: Harper and Row, 1988. Non-Jews in every Nazi-occupied country helped those who were persecuted. Eyewitness accounts, diaries, letters, and memoirs are used to reconstruct the way Jews were helped by people not of their faith.

George Sullivan, *Strange but True Stories of World War II.* New York: Walker, 1983. A recounting of several strange and little-known stories involving WWII. Includes maps and pictures.

MAJOR WORKS CONSULTED

Richard Breitman, *Architect of Genocide: Himmler and the Final Solution.* New York: Alfred A. Knopf, 1991. An exploration of Heinrich Himmler's role in Hitler's Final Solution.

John Devaney, *Hitler: Mad Dictator of World War II.* New York: G.P. Putnam's Sons, 1978. An easy-to-read biography of Adolf Hitler that provides a background on Hitler and offers glimpses of the highlights of his life.

Klaus P. Fischer, *Nazi Germany: A New History.* New York: Continuum, 1995. A comprehensive history that delves deeply into a spectrum of topics relating to Nazi Germany. It presents in a new way Hitler's personality, the early Nazi movement, and the repercussions stemming from Germany's darkest days.

Martin Gilbert, *The Holocaust: A History of the Jews of Europe During the Second World War.* New York: Holt, Rinehart, and Winston, 1985. The definitive account of the systemic attempt to destroy all European Jews that occurred between June 1941 and May 1945. Written by one of England's most distinguished historians.

Helmut Heiber, *Goebbels.* Trans. John K. Dickinson. New York: Hawthorne Books, 1972. A translated biography of Goebbels, one of Hitler's early henchmen, by a leading researcher at the Institute of Contemporary History in Munich, Germany.

Adolf Hitler, *Mein Kampf.* Trans. Roger Manheim. Boston: Houghton Mifflin, 1971. Everything Hitler said he would do he wrote about first in *Mein Kampf.* This is a translated version of the "Nazi Bible" in which Hitler lays out his ideas on race, living space, and conquering the world.

Robert Holland, *Adolf Hitler: A Biography.* New York: Thor, 1966. A very old yet very readable biography of Adolf Hitler that delves into background and ancillary information in a very understandable manner.

Louis C. Kilzer, *Churchill's Deception: The Dark Secret That Destroyed Nazi Germany.* New York: Simon and Schuster, 1994. The story, by a Pulitzer Prize–winning journalist, of how Winston Churchill outsmarted Adolf Hitler into invading the Soviet Union. This has been called one of the darkest secrets of World War II.

H.W. Koch, *The Hitler Youth: Origins and Development 1922–1945.* New York: Stein and Day, 1975. For Hitler's Third Reich to extend for one thousand years, Nazi youth had to be won over to the Nazi cause. This book documents the Hitler Youth movement that primed Germany's children for life in the Third Reich.

Roger Manvell and Heinrich Fraenkel, *Dr. Goebbels: His Life and Death*. New York: Simon and Schuster, 1960. Goebbels's personal story is entangled with the history of the Third Reich. This is one of the earliest biographies of this complex man. It is based, in part, on Goebbels's diary.

———, *Goering*. New York: Simon and Schuster, 1962. The earliest biographical source of the Reich minister is used in this collective biography. The authors are authorities on influential people of the Third Reich.

Bruno Manz, *A Mind in Prison: The Memoir of a Son and Soldier of the Third Reich*. Washington, DC: Brassey's, 2000. The author, who joined Hitler Youth at age eleven, relates firsthand the life of young people during Hitler's reign.

Leonard Mosley, *The Reich Marshall: A Biography of Hermann Goering*. Garden City, NY: Doubleday, 1974. The author of this book knew Goering personally; parts of his biography are based on personal memories as well as interviews with other people who knew Goering.

Peter Padfield, *Himmler*. New York: Henry Holt, 1990. An authoritative and exhaustive biography of one of Hitler's most powerful henchmen.

Mordecai Paldiel, *Saving the Jews*. Rockville, MD: Schreiber, 2000. The stories of righteous gentiles who helped Jews throughout Europe are chronicled in this book.

Robert Payne, *The Life and Death of Adolf Hitler*. New York: Praeger, 1973. Written almost thirty years after Hitler's death, this book gives a detailed account of Adolf Hitler at all stages of his life. Includes sketches made by the Fuehrer during World War I and after.

Eileen Pearson, *Hitler's Reich*. St. Paul, MN: Greenhaven Press, 1980. An easy-to-understand book written for young adults that touches on all aspects of Nazi Germany, from Hitler's first days to the end of World War II.

Viktor Reimann, *Goebbels: The Man Who Created Hitler*. Garden City, NY: Doubleday, 1976. The story of how Goebbels rose in the Nazi Party and seized control of the masses. The author was arrested by the Nazis in 1940 and spent five years in Nazi prisons.

Ralf Georg Reuth, *Goebbels*. New York: Harcourt Brace, 1990. Goebbels's diaries, eyewitness accounts, and archival material were used to write this well-researched biography of Hitler's propaganda minister.

Wulf Schwarzwaller, *Rudolph Hess: The Last Nazi*. Bethesda, MD: National Press, 1988. Hess was the longest-living high-ranking Nazi. Although Hess rose in rank to Hitler's deputy, he is most remembered for his May 10, 1941, self-appointed mission of peace. The author has written extensively about Hitler, the Third Reich, and the Holocaust.

William L. Shirer, *The Rise and Fall of the Third Reich: A History of Nazi Germany.* New York: Simon and Schuster, 1960. A classic about Hitler and the Third Reich told by an author who observed firsthand as a journalist the ins and outs of Hitler's Germany.

Bradley F. Smith, *Heinrich Himmler: A Nazi in the Making.* Stanford, CA: Hoover Institution Press, 1971. This work concentrates on Himmler's early days—his childhood and youth and the factors that led up to his joining the Nazi Party.

Louis L. Snyder, *Hitler's Elite: Shocking Profiles of the Reich's Most Notorious Henchmen.* New York: Berkeley Books, 1989. Profiles of nineteen people who guided Hitler's Germany toward its most brutal atrocities. Each profile captures the person in various stages of their life and career as a henchman.

Albert Speer, *Inside the Third Reich: Memories.* New York: Macmillan, 1970. A classic written by Hitler's private architect turned minister of defense who served a twenty-year prison term for his role in the Third Reich. Part of the book was written while he was serving time.

Ian Westwell, *In the Path of Hitler's Third Reich: The Journey from Victory to Defeat.* New York: Gramercy Books, 1998. A wonderful resource in which to follow Hitler's Nazi Germany as it invaded and conquered Europe. The book's many maps allow the reader to follow along Hitler's path.

Robert Wistrich, *Who's Who in Nazi Germany.* New York: Routledge, 1995. The biographies of 350 individuals representing all walks of life, from the elite to the commoner, who had an impact in Nazi Germany. It is written by the chair of modern European Jewish history at Hebrew University.

Michael Berenbaum, *The World Must Know: The History of the Holocaust as Told in the United States Holocaust Memorial Museum.* Boston: Little, Brown, 1993.

Willi A. Boelcke, *The Secret Conferences of Dr. Goebbels: The Nazi Propaganda War 1939–1943.* New York: E.P. Dutton, 1970.

Harold C. Deutsch, *Hitler and His Generals: The Hidden Crisis, January–June 1938.* Minneapolis: University of Minnesota Press, 1974.

Mary Fulbrook, *A Concise History of Germany.* Cambridge, England: Cambridge University Press, 1991.

Martin Gilbert, *Never Again: A History of the Holocaust.* New York: Universe Publishing, 2000.

Daniel Jonah Goldhagen, *Hitler's Willing Executioners: Ordinary Germans and the Holocaust.* New York: Alfred A. Knopf, 1996.

Frederick V. Grunfeld, *The Hitler File: A Social History of Germany and the Nazis 1918–1945.* New York: Random House, 1974.

Sydney Gruson, "Hitler Dead in Chancellery, Nazis Say . . . ," *New York Times,* May 2, 1945.

Edwin P. Hoyt, *Angels of Death: Goering's Luftwaffe.* New York: Tom Doherty Associates, 1994.

Marion A. Kaplan, *Between Dignity and Despair: Jewish Life in Nazi Germany.* New York: Oxford University Press, 1998.

Martin Kitchen, *A World in Flames: A Short History of the Second World War in Europe and Asia 1939–1945.* New York: Longman's Group, 1990.

Stephen and Norbert Lebert, *My Father's Keeper: Children of Nazi Leaders, an Intimate History of Damage and Denial.* New York: Little, Brown, 2000.

Andy Marino, *Herschel: The Boy Who Started World War II.* Boston: Faber and Faber, 1995.

Michael R. Marrus, *The Holocaust in History.* Hanover, NH: University Press of New England, 1987.

Lili Meier, ed., *Auschwitz Album: A Book Based upon an Album Discovered by a Concentration Camp Survivor.* New York: Random House, 1982.

Dalia Ofer and Lenore J. Weitzman, eds., *Women in the Holocaust.* New Haven, CT: Yale University Press, 1998.

Brian Perrett, *A History of Blitzkrieg.* Briarcliff Manor, NY: Stein and Day, 1983.

Sylvia Rothchild, ed., *Voices from the Holocaust.* New York: New American Library, 1981.

Fred Taylor, ed., *The Goebbels Diaries 1939–1941.* New York: G.P. Putnam's Sons, 1983.

Emmy E. Werner, *Through the Eyes of Innocents: Children Witness World War II.* Boulder, CO: Westview Press, 2000.

Wilhelm Wulf, *Zodiac and Swastika: How Astrology Guided Hitler's Germany.* New York: Coward, McCann, and Geoghegan, 1973.

INDEX

111

PICTURE CREDITS

Cover Photos: © Getty Images (upper left and right/center/lower right); © Bettmann/CORBIS (lower left)

© Associated Press, 37, 41, 52, 54, 83

© Austrian Archives/CORBIS, 57

© Bettmann/CORBIS, 11, 42

© Christel Gerstenbergh/CORBIS, 48

© Hulton/Archive by Getty Images, 12, 15, 16, 27, 29, 30, 35, 36, 50, 56, 59, 69, 71, 72, 74, 77, 84

© Hulton-Deutsch Collection/CORBIS, 87

National Archives, 91

© Underwood & Underwood/CORBIS, 89

USHMM Photo Archives, 7, 9, 14, 18, 20, 21, 26, 32, 33, 39, 45, 47, 49, 53, 61, 62, 64, 66, 75, 79, 80, 86, 90, 93

ABOUT THE AUTHOR

Marylou Morano Kjelle is a freelance writer and photojournalist who lives and works in central New Jersey. Marylou writes for several local newspapers and has a column in the *Westfield Leader/Times of Scotch Plains-Fanwood* called the "Children's Book Nook" in which she reviews children's books and writes about the love of reading. She holds an M.S. in science from Rutgers University. Marylou has always had an interest in reading and writing history, and her home in New Jersey is close to the site of a Revolutionary War battle. *Hitler's Henchmen* is her fourth nonfiction book for young readers.